WITHDRAWN

HIGHWAYS OF
CHRISTIAN DOCTRINE

HIGHWAYS OF CHRISTIAN DOCTRINE

BY

SHIRLEY JACKSON CASE

Dean of the Divinity School
University of Chicago

WILLETT, CLARK & COMPANY
CHICAGO   NEW YORK
1936

Copyright 1936 by
WILLETT, CLARK & COMPANY

Manufactured in The U. S. A. by The Plimpton Press
Norwood, Mass.-La Porte, Ind.

PREFACE

This volume contains the Lowell Institute Lectures delivered in King's Chapel, Boston, Massachusetts, April 27 to May 1, 1936. The invitation to give the lectures was accompanied by a request that they sketch broadly the changes through which Christian doctrines have passed from their beginnings to the present time.

Everyone knows that the first Christians did not discourse long and learnedly on elaborate doctrinal issues. In this respect they stand in striking contrast to many of their distinguished successors. Imagine the impatience, if not the bewilderment, of Peter or James had either attempted to read Origen's *De principiis*, Augustine's *De trinitate,* the *Summa* of Thomas Aquinas, or Calvin's *Institutio*. Certainly the leaders of the early church would have been sad misfits among the theologians who assembled in council at Nicea, Chalcedon or Trent. And how incongruous it would have been to ask Peter and his associates to subscribe to either the Augsburg or the Westminster Confession!

How has it come about that the once unadorned faith of the original disciples of Jesus has grown through the centuries into the mass of varied and complex doctrinal statements embodied in the creeds and confessions of the historic church and advocated by successive generations of professional theologians? This is the question we have attempted to answer.

The lecturer takes this opportunity to express his thanks to the officials of the Lowell Institute who sponsored the course and to the audiences who gave his message so kind a reception.

SHIRLEY JACKSON CASE

Divinity School
University of Chicago

CONTENTS

LECTURE ONE

◆

THE ASCENT TO PHILOSOPHY

The followers of Jesus who assembled in Jerusalem after his crucifixion were ardent revivalists. They summoned their hearers to repent in preparation for the imminent dawn of a new age to be inaugurated by the heaven-exalted Christ. This conviction so thoroughly possessed them that they felt no need to justify their opinions at the bar of cold reason. Christian enthusiasm had not yet experienced the restraints later to be imposed upon it by institutional controls and the rigors of logic.

The members of the primitive Christian community performed the task for which they were best fitted by heritage, disposition and environment. In no respect were they trained theological scholars. Even had they so desired, they could hardly have propounded a comprehensive and carefully articulated scheme of doctrine. Their discipline had been of quite another sort. They were skilled in casting the fisherman's net or in wielding the tools of the common laborer; they had no standing within the learned professions of their day. Judged by the educational norms of their contemporaries, they were unschooled peasants who spoke a Galilean patois that marked them off as rustics in the sight of the aristocratic element in the population of metropolitan Jerusalem. Their social and cultural antecedents were rural, provincial and unacademic.

Happily for the health of society, moral sincerity and religious zeal do not always wait upon the findings of the learned. These virtues are sometimes conspicuously displayed by persons subject to strong emotions. Temperamentally they are impulsive rather than deliberate, their activities are determined by waves of feeling rather than by sober judgments and they are unsuited to the pursuit of philosophy. On the other hand, the emotionally activated individual can be very serviceable in the launching of reforms, in the advocacy of worthy but unpopular causes, or in the liberation of moral and spiritual energy when its vitality is menaced by the inertia of ancient customs and sanctified establishments.

It is one of their chief distinctions that the earliest Christians espoused a unique way of living inspired by an ethically and religiously motivated enthusiasm. They embodied in their life as a group and advocated among their Jewish kinsmen a new form of specialization in righteousness. While they intended no disloyalty to their ancestral heritage, the past concerned them less than did recent events in their own experience and their expectation of still more marvelous things to occur in the near future. They lived for a glorious tomorrow when Jesus would return in triumph to pass judgment upon sinners and reward the righteous. This vivid imagery controlled their thinking and shaped their conduct. With singleness of purpose, proclaiming their faith in the risen Jesus, they admonished their hearers to repent and join the company of his followers in order to be ready for the reception of the Messiah when he should appear.

The first Christians exemplified a distinctly Jewish type of piety phrased in a pictorial imagery characteristically employed by the Hebrews. Doctrine was essentially a bold assertion of faith that did not need to be justified by processes of human reasoning. Its truth was guaranteed by a revelation so overwhelmingly convincing that apologetic arguments on its behalf were entirely unnecessary. Belief in Jesus' resurrection and ascent to heaven rested on the testimony of those who confidently affirmed that they had seen him alive again after the crucifixion. They felt no need to defend the intellectual propriety of their faith. Two centuries were to elapse before the advocates of Christianity learned to adopt the procedure, already current among the Greeks, of arranging ideas into an integrated scheme of logically validated opinion. Sometime between the years 220 and 230 A.D. Origen, a teacher in Alexandria, published the first systematic treatise on Christian doctrine. The Christian mind had spent nearly two hundred years in making its journey from the intellectual lowlands of simple Jewish piety to the first conspicuous station on the rising slopes of Greek philosophical wisdom.

I

Progress at first was painfully slow. At only one point had primitive Christian thinking diverged radically from current Jewish notions. That was the belief that Jesus, a crucified man, had been inducted by God into the office of future Messianic redeemer. All else was taken over essentially unchanged from contemporary Palestinian Judaism.

God and the cosmos were pictured in genuinely Jewish fashion, Jerusalem was the place where the Messiah would appear to set up his kingdom, final salvation was to be realized in fulfillment of the covenant made by God with the ancestors of the Jews, the ancient Scriptures were the infallible source of divine revelation, and the Holy Spirit that had inspired the prophets of old spoke again through enthusiastic Christian evangelists. Hebrew religion was thought to have advanced one step nearer to completion through the activities of Jesus' followers.

Perhaps it was fortunate for their peace of mind that the earliest Christians could not foresee the future course of events by which they and their successors were to be forced again and again to rethink the meaning of their message and task. They waited in vain for the triumphant return of Jesus " in the glory of his Father with the holy angels " to deliver Palestine from the Romans. In the meantime overzealous Jewish nationalists instigated a political revolution that resulted in the destruction of their temple in 70 A.D. and the necessary withdrawal of the Christian group from Jerusalem as the center of its activity. The evangelistic propaganda in Palestine, having yielded only meager results, had been so rephrased by some of its advocates within a year or two after Jesus' death that a few Jews of the Dispersion found it acceptable. But not until it was further recast to meet the needs of Gentiles did it gain a substantial following. Then Gentiles themselves took in hand the task of giving Christian doctrine a form suitable to their situations in Ephesus or Alexandria or Rome, where the Christian congregations asserted their complete severance from Judaism and claimed to represent the true religion designed by God to become the peculiar possession of Gentiles.

The geographical, political and social conditions that shaped the course of the Christian movement's history during the first and second centuries compelled corresponding changes in doctrine. Its advocates were forced to choose a new highway for the routing of their thought. Delay in Jesus' expected return, the necessity of abandoning Palestine as Christianity's specific provenance, and the general refusal of the Jews to ally themselves with the new sect, were facts that struck at the very foundations of the only distinctive item in early Christian doctrine. Had not the reverence paid to the risen Jesus been misplaced? He did not return in triumph, he did not establish the Kingdom of God in Palestine, he did not deliver the Jewish people from their distresses. One might easily have inferred that the central Christian doctrine preached by the first disciples had been completely exploded by the actual outcome of historical events.

Christian thinking had now to make a choice between two alternatives. Either it might abandon its original contention that Jesus was deserving of unique allegiance, or it might seek to discover new ways of justifying this confidence. The latter course was the one chosen, and for many years to come the principal items stressed in the growth of Christian doctrine centered about this all-important theme. Attention might shift from the post-resurrection glory of Jesus to his display of divine power and wisdom while on earth, or to his pre-existent dignity in the Godhead, in accordance with changing conditions of thinking, but the creative urge to make Jesus worthy of believers' reverence remained constant.

Thus the chief concern of Christian thinkers was their doctrine of Christ, that is, " Christology," rather than their doctrine of God, which is " theology " in the stricter sense of that term. They accepted without question Jewish teaching about God and promulgated it essentially unchanged in their preaching to Gentiles. But their doctrine about Christ was an original contribution that had to be made and re-made in response to new demands and in accordance with the intellectual abilities of Christian thinkers. Earlier notions regarding the significance of Christ were not immediately abandoned. But gradually they were revised or supplemented until in the end they bore only slight resemblance to their original form and largely lost their primitive content. Yet throughout this process of change, reverence for the hero of the faith remained the guiding star of the interpreter.

Pauline Christology is a striking illustration of one early attempt to revise Christian thinking. Paul accepted wholeheartedly the Christological beliefs of his Palestinian Christian predecessors. He unhesitatingly affirmed that the crucified Jesus had been exalted to a position of Messianic dignity in heaven whence he would presently descend to execute judgment and assemble his followers into the fellowship of the new Kingdom of God to be established on the earth. Gentile converts were warned that the Lord is at hand; they were encouraged to maintain an attitude of momentary expectation, they were admonished to live with the imminent day of judgment ever in mind, and at each celebration of their religious meal they pledged anew their faith in Christ's advent. This type of imagery recurs again and again in Paul's correspondence with different Christian groups, but it represents only one phase of Pauline Christology.

Paul found himself from time to time in situations that stimulated other ways of thinking about Christ. By the year 50 he had virtually abandoned efforts to convert Jews. Leaving this task to his more conservatively minded fellow laborers, like Peter and Barnabas, Paul devoted himself specifically to the winning of Gentiles. But evidently he assumed that this emphasis involved no essential change in his Christian doctrine. In Thessalonica, one of the earliest scenes of his activity on European soil, he had preached his familiar Jewish-Christian message calling for the renunciation of idolatry and belief in the Son of God who had suffered death, who had arisen and ascended into heaven, and who would presently return to earth to inaugurate the day of judgment (I Thess. 1:9f.). The distinctively Christian part of this message was the appeal for loyalty to Christ in the role of a heroic redeemer after the pattern of Jewish apocalypticism. Was it not folly for Paul to assume that this eminently Jewish way of thinking would prove at all acceptable to Gentiles?

Paul freely admits that when he arrived in Corinth he was in a discouraged frame of mind. In this important Greek city he began his preaching "in fear and in much trembling." He does not divulge the cause of his anxiety. But if, as his biographer in the Book of Acts recounts, he had attempted to convert those reputed experts in Greek wisdom known as philosophers, he soon discovered the futility of his effort. It was useless to talk to them about accepting the tribal God of the Hebrews in preference to their supreme deity, even though the latter might be called by many names. It was equally impossible to persuade them to believe in a resurrection of the dead and a cataclysmic day of judgment. Paul was incapable of transforming the picturesque Christology of primitive Christianity into a philosophical dogma. Another century of history had to intervene before this metamorphosis could be successfully accomplished.

Paul wisely decided to address himself to the uneducated classes, among whom he aimed to arouse an enthusiasm for Christ that would be as satisfactory for the Gentiles as it had been for the first Palestinian believers. In this effort he was eminently successful, but the practical demands of the situation involved some radical alterations in earlier ways of thinking about Christ and his significance. Paul may not have perceived beforehand all that was involved. When he decided that " Jesus Christ and him crucified " should be presented to the Corinthians as the central figure expressing " God's wisdom in a mystery," the stage was set for an interpretation of Christ in line with a widely prevalent type of popular religious thinking among Gentiles.

Belief in a future triumph of Christ and the evidential value of his post-resurrection appearance were not discarded, for Gentiles themselves knew something of the hope for a new age and they were even more ready than Jews to accept the possibility of divine apparitions. But Gentile heroic redeemers, who had met death triumphantly, were commonly thought to be more immediately serviceable to their devotees in this present life-situation. Instead of waiting to demonstrate their beneficent lordship through some catastrophic event in the future, they displayed their favor and power as lords over the present community of worshipers. In the rites of initiation and the ceremonies of the cult one realized emotionally the help of the divinity and thus accounted him a present savior.

To what extent Paul would have admitted that his Christological thinking had been reshaped under the direct influence of his Gentile surroundings may be open to question. But there can be no doubt of the fact that he tremendously enhanced the prestige of his Christ among the common people of Corinth when he allowed them to believe that baptism into the name of Christ inseparably united them to their Savior, that they participated in his body and blood at the celebration of the Lord's Supper, that he dwelt in their bodies as a spiritual presence requiring moral purity in living, and that in their activities as a worshiping group they were the " body of Christ and severally members thereof." The Lord Jesus Christ now presided over and dwelt in his devotees as individuals and as a community. He was virtually the only God needed by the devout and unlearned Gentile Christians. Undoubtedly reverence for him was felt to be sufficiently justified by present experiences of his divine power quite apart from the verifiability of traditional testimonies to his post-resurrection appearances or his ultimate fulfillment of Jewish apocalyptic expectations.

II

A very different way of justifying faith in Christ was pursued by still other early Christians. Apparently it had not occurred to Paul to cite events in the earthly career of Jesus in support of reverence for the heaven-exalted Christ. While Paul had ascribed to Jesus a pre-earthly existence in which he had been virtually the equal of God in dignity and authority, his career on earth was assumed to have been one of exemplary servant-like humility, for which God had rewarded him with the honors of a new Messianic Lordship in heaven after the crucifixion (Phil. 2:5-11). To other thinkers, if they were at all aware of this Pauline notion, it seemed that one important highway to a more adequate appreciation of Christ had been missed. When they undertook to explore this path they were led to the discovery of many features in Jesus' earthly career that supplied valuable credentials in support of later Christological doctrine. The results of this effort, in various stages of its development, are recorded in the several gospel narratives.

Jesus, it was recalled, had possessed on earth a unique spiritual endowment equipping him to work miracles and cast out demons, thereby demonstrating his superiority over Satan, the prince of the powers of darkness. The words of Jesus also bore witness to his divine authority. He quite overshadowed Moses, by whom God had revealed his will to the Hebrews in earlier times. Jesus was also a prophet who fulfilled in his career the predictions recorded in Scripture and forecast still more significant happenings to occur in the future. He announced, sometimes in a veiled manner and sometimes explicitly, the fact of his own Messiahship. Two of the evangelists were able to report that he had been miraculously born, thus making his entry into the world a fitting prelude to his initial Messianic work while on earth and its consummation in events to happen after his death. Thus Christ's title to respect was demonstrated by historical portraiture rather than by the immediacy of mystical experience that had characterized the Pauline type of interpretation.

The needs of the continuing Christian movement gradually made more evident the necessity for Christian thinking to strike its roots more deeply into history. The passing of time slowly dulled interest in the future redemptive activity of Christ, but this loss was less keenly felt when his saving power could be attested by the personal feelings of every worshiper at the present moment. Individual emotions were, however, a precarious foundation on which to rear a substantial community life. Even in Paul's day the disruptive effects of spirit-prompted individualism and its menace to the solidarity of the Christian group had become apparent. Since the great need now was standardized guidance and authentic controls, thinking about Christ took on new meaning when it was perceived that he, by virtue of his superior foresight and solicitous concern for the welfare of his followers, had provided beforehand for these necessities. Thus Christology became institutionalized and, conversely, the practical worth of the growing ecclesiastical machinery reinforced the truth of the Christian doctrine.

Henceforth Christ figured pre-eminently as the founder and sustainer of the new Christian society. He was the historic author of the developing organization and the guarantor of its saving efficacy. He had authorized apostles and their successors to be its presiding officials, had ordained its sacred rites and insured their sacramental validity. By his fulfillment of ancient prophecy he had made the Hebrew Scriptures a rightful possession of the church, and by his own words and deeds he had added the final supplement to the ancient revelation. The afflictions endured by Christians were but a repetition of experiences like those through which he had passed. Even persecution unto death, which for the faithful meant simply punishment for their allegiance to the name of Christ, was endured in the confidence that he had been the ideal martyr. Loyalty to him and loyalty to the church had become synonymous. And a satisfying sense of immediacy in the believer's relation to Christ was obtainable only through membership in the divine society that he had founded.

In religion, as in other areas of human interest, most persons covet the sense of safety that is gained by trust in the efficacy of a standardized mechanism of administration, in preference to reliance upon the uncertain possibilities of individual effort. Religious enthusiasm, like the zeal of a mob, thrives best under the inspiration of the crowd. But this inspiration tends quickly to evaporate when the crowd disbands, unless some more tangible and permanent instrument is devised to give it coherence and stability. Wise church-men, like astute politicians, readily come to appreciate the value of an organization to symbolize, implement and safe-guard the will and the welfare of the group. Then, almost immediately, as the concrete embodiment of the idealized cause, the organization acquires sanctity in its own right. Its constitution and bylaws become authoritative norms for the thinking and conduct of all its members.

When doctrines have become thus institutionalized, al-terations in their form or content are exceedingly difficult to effect. Proposed changes seem to reflect discredit not only upon the validity of traditional beliefs but also upon the de-pendability of the institution by which they have been sponsored. Whether it is a creed of state or church that is called in question, the rank and file in the group have too large a stake in the established order to admit the propriety of tampering with its doctrinal foundations. Individual thinkers who detect flaws and advocate corrections are viewed with suspicion or alarm. The value of new ideas is not to be judged simply on the strength of their claim to inherent validity, but in relation to the welfare of the exist-ing organization. Personal initiative can be tolerated or prized only in so far as it serves, or seems to serve, the gen-eral good. If it appears to deviate therefrom, its representa-tives are criticized or disciplined and, if incorrigible, are expelled.

The psychology of institutionalism became a very potent factor in shaping the course of Christian thinking during the second century. In this period the church as an organization developed several definitive characteristics. Episcopal government became more widely established, social solidarity was further cemented by successive conflicts with the secular authorities, the activities of the worshiping congregations took on the character of ritual ceremonies, significant progress was made toward the establishment of a New Testament canon of Scripture, and beliefs crystallized into dogmatic formulas like the so-called Apostles' Creed. At the same time the church was constantly adding to its membership new converts who represented an ever widening range of individual tastes, interests, temperaments and cultural heritages. While institutional consolidation moved in the direction of uniformity, increases in personnel tended toward greater diversity.

Two divergent ways of arriving at Christian truth were clearly evident in this situation. From the institution's point of view the ultimate test of valid doctrine was conformity to approved tradition, an unquestioning acceptance of " the faith which was once for all delivered to the saints." On the other hand, the individual thinker sought the kind of truth that could command his personal intellectual approval. In the last resort his appeal was to the philosopher's criterion, however slow and uncertain his footsteps might be along the highway traveled by the more distinguished Gentile thinkers of that day. The Christian philosopher might boldly venture to substitute knowledge for faith, or his intellectual urge might content itself with the less perilous task of defending, supplementing and reinterpreting tradition. While proceeding thus without giving offense, he might be lauded as a faithful apologist for the church. Neither he nor his associates perceived the extent to which he was actually effecting significant transformations in doctrine as he shaped it to his personal liking. But if he were less ardent in his defense of tradition, he might so stress new ways of thinking that they would be adjudged by his less venturesome contemporaries a menace to both the authority and stability of the ecclesiastical institution within which his novel ideas sought a home. In the latter event the advocate of new opinions encountered opposition, lost caste in the group, and suffered the fate of the heretic.

III

Late in the first century, or early in the second, the author of the Gospel of John displayed at least a faltering inclination to tread the philosophical path. He initiated a type of Christological speculation in which reverence for the hero of Christian faith was provided with strikingly new supports. At the very outset Christ was declared to have been the incarnation of the Logos, the Christianized counterpart of the Divine Reason that for centuries had figured conspicuously in certain types of Greek philosophical speculation. The distinctive credential of Jesus consisted in the fact that he brought from above into this lower world a fresh revelation of enlightening truth by virtue of which he became the Savior for all those who accepted the revelation. Thus Jesus was the Messiah whom God had sent not only to redeem the Jews, by whom he had been generally rejected, but also to be the Savior of all mankind. Salvation, to be realized through this divine enlightenment, was unavailable for those whose minds remained so dark that they refused to receive the light of truth personified in Christ.

Like Paul's Lord of the worshiping community, the Johannine Savior confers his benefits here and now. His future advent thus becomes even less important than it was for Paul. One now learns that the primary purpose of Jesus had not been to inaugurate ultimately an apocalyptic regime but to found a kingdom of truth. Saving knowledge of Christ is an immediate personal possession of every member of the church in fulfillment of the promise made by Jesus that after his death the Comforter, who is the spirit of truth, would come to lead the faithful into all truth. This attainment is fundamentally an affair of the individual and its acquisition is mystically realized. But, again, the Johannine mysticism is very different from the Pauline. In the latter the believer possesses Christ as a substantial element in his being, while in the former he is an increment of knowledge resident in the mind. In the one case the type of mysticism represented may be termed " ontological " and in the other, " epistemological."

Resort to mysticism saved the Johannine author from any conscious break, either in principle or in fact, with the church as an institution. Since knowledge pertained chiefly to the supra-mundane and subjective realms, it did not yield a set of logical conclusions that had to be applied concretely to the criticism or elimination of specific items in current tradition. He affirmed the absolute necessity of baptism and participation in the Lord's Supper. These rites were to be performed with literal accuracy. Probably even thus early in the history of the church it would have been thought an unpardonable sin to cast suspicion upon the efficacy of the sacraments. But newly apprehended truth, without being at all antagonistic to tradition, might properly serve an enriching and enlightening purpose. The alternative of baptism by water or by the spirit of knowledge was not proposed, but the necessity of both was affirmed. The communicant must also eat the flesh and drink the blood of Jesus at the eucharistic meal, and at the same time participate in the knowledge which Christ came down from heaven to reveal. One could with propriety tell the Jews that knowledge of Christian truth was alone sufficient to liberate them from bondage to their racial past, if immediately one testified to Abraham's knowledge of Christ and thereby saved for the church the sanctity of its ancient Scriptures. The Christian thinker who was thus loyal to the ecclesiastical institution could be as original as he pleased in his personal opinions.

Not all Christians were content to maintain the Johannine moderation. During the first half of the second century Christ in his role of revealer of new knowledge was so highly exalted by one school of thought that it threatened to undermine the whole ecclesiastical superstructure of the day. These disturbers of Christianity's doctrinal peace were the so-called Gnostics.

Gnosticism was already a distinct type of religious philosophy before it invaded Christian circles. It was one of those speculative aberrations common in that age. Logical

thinking had been far more self-exacting in the days of
Plato and Aristotle than it was in Roman imperial times.
In the course of the years philosophy had abandoned the seclusion of the cloister to parade the streets and dispense its
benefits over mankind at large. Nor was it any longer the
métier of the select few, pursuing truth strictly for truth's
sake. Rather, it had become a missionary propaganda that
sought to make truth — or a particular school's version of
the truth — a genuine gospel capable of securing to the aver-
age man present peace of mind and release from future
anxiety. More people indulged in thinking, or thought they
thought — which amounted to the same thing so far as their
personal satisfactions were concerned. Like a nugget of gold
removed from the secret chamber of a vault and beat into
gold-leaf to adorn the cupolas of public buildings, philosophy
became a delight to the eyes of the multitude. What was
lost in depth and concentration was compensated for by
gains in popularity and spaciousness. Often the intellectual
veneer was rather thin, but its therapeutic value was none
the less generally appreciated.

In line with this utilitarian trend, Gnostic thinking was
essentially a program for saving man's soul. Thus religion
was the fundamental concern of the Gnostics, while their
interest in philosophy was not an end in itself but only the
means of attaining to a more ultimate goal. They found no
difficulty in appropriating varied items from current schools
of thought in so far as these contributed to the solution of
their religious problem. Nor did they feel it compulsory to
follow in detail the complete system of any particular school.

Thus on becoming acquainted with Christianity they were quite ready to accept its traditional opinions when these met their needs and to reject the rest as unnecessary or untrue.

Gnosticism, being a frontal attack on the problem of evil, found the Christian idea of Christ the Savior exceedingly attractive. This was especially true of the Pauline and Johannine representation that Christ was a pre-existent divine being who had descended from the realm of the supreme God to bring deliverance to needy mortals. Platonic transcendentalism was already a prominent item in the syncretism of the Gnostics. They posited an upper world of pure spiritual being out of which the soul of man had descended, or been lured, to become helplessly entangled in the snares of this evil lower world. Oriental dualism had also heightened the note of desperation in Gnostic thinking by alleging the inherently evil character of material being from which the soul needed deliverance. Therefore to make salvation possible it was necessary that new redeeming power should descend out of the pure spirit-world above to help the distressed soul escape from its unfortunate plight.

Before coming into contact with Christianity Gnostic thinkers had not succeeded in working out an entirely satisfactory theory of the concrete means by which the necessary saving help was mediated. The figure of the Christian Redeemer seemed to meet admirably this need. Hence he was ardently accepted, especially by energetic Gnostics in Alexandria who joined the Christian movement during the early part of the second century. As the name by which they have become generally known implies, they were primarily interested in knowledge (*gnosis*) and only secondarily in the church as an institution. They were not, however, anti-ecclesiastical. They were devout worshipers who cultivated the mystical type of religious experience. But their philosophical bent was sufficiently strong to lead them to question the validity of certain items in traditional thinking heretofore generally approved by churchmen.

One logical consequence of Gnostic dualism was a deprecatory judgment upon all materiality. Matter was essentially and irredeemably bad; spirit alone was divine and salvable. Hence the Jewish-Christian doctrine of a resurrection of the flesh was summarily dismissed. The redeemed soul needed to be completely released from the body; a reincarnation would involve it again in troubles and defilements. If Christ were a genuine Savior the doctrine of his earthly incarnation had to be held rather loosely, if not denied outright, in the interests of preserving the purity and efficiency of his person and message. Baptism and the eucharist were merely symbolic acts, if indeed they had any value. It was thought a gross absurdity to speak literally of eating the body and drinking the blood of Christ.

Even the God of the Old Testament did not escape the damaging attacks of Gnostic logic. Since, according to the Scriptures, he had created this material world, either he was himself an evil power or else he was an inferior divinity perhaps unaware of the futility of his work. And if this were true, the Scriptures could not be the final and infallible revelation of the Supreme Deity. Nor could they forecast perfectly the work of Christ and guarantee the security and authority of the church. On the contrary, Christ had brought a distinctly new revelation superior to, if not wholly independent of, the Hebrew Scriptures. The elucidation of this new knowledge was the peculiar task of the Gnostic teacher.

At one point the loyal churchman and the Gnostic Christian occupied common ground. Both revered Christ the Savior. But they diverged widely in their views on the meaning of salvation and the proper technique for its realization. The churchman trusted in his divine institution through whose sacred traditions and holy sacraments Christ ministered to the needs of the total body of initiates. The Gnostic, on the other hand, was essentially an educationalist preaching a gospel for the elect few who would respond to the appeal of the teacher and individually attain unto a mystico-philosophical knowledge of Christ. In principle the two methods were diametrically opposed to each other.

The Gnostic schools waged an unequal conflict with the Christian ecclesiastical establishment. Gnosticism, deficient as it was in institutional strength, was doomed to defeat from the start. But the victor learned some useful lessons from his valiant foe. Not the least was a clearer apprehension of the necessity to frame a more effective apologetic for the affirmations on which the structure of the historic church had been reared. Otherwise organized Christianity could not hope to hold the allegiance of educated and cultured people. Christian thinkers must learn to tread more diligently, if also more cautiously, the philosophic path.

IV

Many difficulties obstructed the way of a theologian who attempted to serve acceptably the cause of the church and at the same time win the confidence of his more thoughtful contemporaries. Gentile philosophical schools on the one hand, and traditional Christianity on the other, bequeathed their respective heritages to the apologist. He could not discard outright these impedimenta and maintain his dignity among his fellow travelers. Porters and hotel clerks are not the only people who base opinions about the excursionist on the stylishness of his luggage. The would-be Christian philosopher had to be so accoutred, both as thinker and as churchman, that he could make Christianity intellectually respectable and make philosophy ecclesiastically acceptable. And, strange as it may seem, it appears to have been an easier task to make Christians out of pagan intellectuals than it was to make philosophers out of churchmen.

Changes had been taking place among Greek philosophers themselves that rendered Christianity more appealing. Epicureanism and Skepticism had given way to other schools that concerned themselves more with a moral and religious view of the world. Stoicism had ceased to deal extensively in dialectics, but continued to preach moral virtues and divine immanence. The revival of Platonic transcendentalism, which made the quest for knowledge of God the very core of philosophical endeavor, was rapidly gaining favor. And there was a growing tendency among many intellectuals to seek in some accepted authority a resting place for thought and a release from the rigors of logic. Christianity had several attractions to offer in this setting. It claimed to possess knowledge of the only true and supreme Deity. Its moral ideals were strenuous and noble. And it justified its teaching by reference to the concrete authority of its Scriptures for which it affirmed both divine inspiration and unsurpassable antiquity. Had Christianity set itself up as simply a school of philosophy, emphasizing only these features in its teaching, undoubtedly it would have secured a large following from among the educated classes of the day.

Christianity now was also — and primarily — a religious cult. Resistance to the Gnostics had made it perfectly evident that Christianity was to remain a cult. The church, which perpetuated the practices and traditions of the cult, took precedence over any thinkers who might attempt to expound its doctrines. In some quarters all philosophers were suspect; it was felt that however docile they might be they could find no place in the church. This prejudice was a result of unhappy experience with the Gnostic extremists. Even a man of Tertullian's learning, great as was his personal debt to Stoicism, spurned a " mottled Christianity " compounded of Platonic, Aristotelian and Stoic ingredients. But this hostile temper could not prevail. Converted philosophers, pressing their way into the church, rendered it valuable service. Previously they had studied in various schools of contemporary thought, but now they devoted their talents and learning to the cause of Christianity. Other scholars, growing up within the church, deliberately familiarized themselves with the wisdom of the Greeks as a means of increasing their Christian efficiency. The church needed these leaders to guide it along the road to intellectual respectability.

Christian scholars concentrated their efforts upon one chief task. They strove to demonstrate that Christianity, when properly understood, was the proponent of the highest form of philosophical wisdom. By way of illustration one needs only to recall the work of intellectuals like Justin Martyr, Clement of Alexandria and Origen. As they conceived their mission, it was not to transform Christianity into a new philosophical movement, but to persuade their contemporaries that the church was the place wherein the best minds of the age could fittingly exercise their skill by defending and elaborating the traditional affirmations of the Christian faith. This truce between the church and Greek philosophy was so one-sided that it might almost be termed a complete surrender on the part of the latter. In capitulating, philosophy had lost its suzerainty; yet it had not been entirely shorn of its dignity and influence. The result was highly significant for the further progress of Christian doctrine. We shall note only the most important consequences.

The philosopher in the church gave Christianity its first real doctrine of God — its first " God-ology " — comparable in importance to its already conspicuous Christology. Orthodox Christians had always believed in the one true God who had revealed himself to the Hebrews. Loyalty to him was professed in a baptismal formula that seems to have been widely current by the close of the first century. Also the oldest conventionalized creed, expressing reaction to Gnostic doubts on the subject, gave first place to " One God,

Father Almighty" who, as Irenaeus declared, "made heaven and earth and all things that are therein." To this faith everyone gave assent. It was the password to membership in the church, the initial step toward union with Christ as Savior-God, and the passport to heaven. But Irenaeus spoke only the language of the cleric concerned to maintain the validity of his cult. It remained the task of the Christian philosophers to present reasoned arguments for belief in God, and to define his nature and attributes.

Greek philosophers had long been accustomed to discourse at length about God. Transcendentalism, then popular, required that God should be "totally other" — to adopt a phrase that is often on the lips of a certain type of theologian in our day. But in the opinion of the ancient thinker, this quality of "otherness" was due to the absolutely infinite and purely incorporeal constitution of deity, rather than to the hopeless status of man in this present evil world. The Gnostics had worked from the latter premise, but their theory had been scorned by the church. Hence the new generation of Christian theologians approached their problem from a more strictly metaphysical point of view. In contrast to the finite and transitory nature of all things connected with this world of sense, God was the incomprehensible, the infinite, the immovable, the impassible, the ineffable and the ultimately spiritual essence. Teaching about the Deity now became a fundamental theme and furnished the point of departure for discussion of other items in the total scheme of Christian thinking. Christ no longer overshadowed God in the realm of doctrinal discussion. Thus

Origen made God the subject of the opening chapter in his treatise on systematic theology, a procedure that has been followed ever since in standard works on Christian doctrine.

A second important consequence of introducing philosophy into Christian theology was the new turn given to Christological thinking. Unlike the Gnostics, the new intellectual leaders within Christianity were essentially optimistic in their view of the present material world. It was a creation of the Supreme Deity, however much it might have suffered from invasion by hostile forces of evil. Being loyal churchmen, they accepted the authority of the Scriptures in which they read that the creator had looked upon the work of his hands and pronounced it very good. Nor had it ever been without his protecting care. But how could a transcendental Deity, an absolutely incorporeal Spirit, be thus realistically involved in material existence and linked up with the processes of human history? The problem was solved by making Christ the agent of God in creation and in all his subsequent relations with the world. Through Christ's mediation the Hebrews had received their unique revelation, and Greek wisdom, in so far as it was valuable, had also been derived from the same source. All of the dealings of the Deity with the world and mankind had been carried on by Christ, who was identified fully with the divine Logos. Thus Christ became thoroughly deified — a "second God" they sometimes said — without dethroning the Hebrew Deity, as the Gnostics had done. The popular reverential imagery, long employed in the ceremonies of the cult to sustain faith in Christ the Savior, was now supplemented by the intellectual justification of the theologian who could have declared, in Ritschlian phrase, that Christ had the full value of God for the world and mankind from the beginning of creation to the end of time.

Again, the church was heavily indebted to its philosophers for giving intellectual respectability to its Scriptures. Greeks, accustomed as they were to justify their opinions by reference to the ancient poets and philosophers, already possessed a habit of mind that cleared the way for an acceptance of the Scriptures if any Christian was sufficiently appreciative of Greek wisdom to compare it respectfully with that of Moses. Christian scholars now took this step, at the same time pointing to the greater antiquity of Moses, his more immediate connection with the one true God who is the source of all wisdom, and the dependability of Scripture as attested by the abundant fulfillments of the prophecies therein recorded. Some of these Christian interpreters were adepts in the art of allegorical exposition, a method well known to the Greeks as a means of justifying modern opinions by reference to ancient documents. The sacred books of the church could now be revered as a body of divine wisdom and accepted in full confidence by every intelligent person whose eyes were opened to perceive their real meaning. The gospel dictum that God's truth had been hidden from the wise and learned and revealed unto babes was thus completely reversed. The babes might be saved through the simple exercise of faith, but the educated Christians, and only they, could plumb the depths of true knowledge.

In their stress on knowledge as necessary to the highest

type of religion, these scholars within the church made still another significant contribution to Christianity. They were at heart educationalists and placed the profession of teacher on a par with, if not indeed above, that of priest. They were preachers and prophets of truth rather than ministers of a cult. They had no desire to magnify this distinction or to exalt their work above that of the regular clergy. But they clearly elevated human reason to a position of new dignity within Christianity without precipitating an open conflict between faith and knowledge. The highest type of piety could not be realized merely through acceptance of authority and the practice of ritual conformity, necessary as these things were. One must recognize also a moral duty to understand truth; progress in Christian living led ever forward towards more complete knowledge. Mysticism was not rejected, and to some of these intellectuals it seems to have been rather congenial, but they all pressed beyond both simple faith and epistemological mysticism toward the more strenuous task of learning to do right and think right as a personal responsibility of the intelligent individual. Christian doctrine was not merely a set of beliefs to be blindly accepted, even though in one's religious childhood, so to speak, the church was entered in this manner. But growth in virtue demanded progress in learning. Faith itself was increased by the acquisition of knowledge and the enlargement of one's vision of truth attainable only through the pursuit of rationally acquired wisdom.

Proceeding along this pathway Christian thinking had at last come to terms — terms largely of its own making —

with Greek philosophy. Generally speaking, it was the method rather than the content of philosophy that had been appropriated. The discovery of truth in its most complete form had become the personal responsibility of the individual thinker who supplemented without opposing ecclesiastical tradition and practice. The church remained the mistress while philosophy became the handmaid. With impunity Justin could declare it to be " in fact the greatest and most honorable possession in the sight of God, to whom it alone leads and unites us; and they are truly holy who have given attention to philosophy." Clement made similar affirmations without jeopardizing his standing in the Alexandrian church. Philosophy, he said, had been a schoolmaster to bring the Greeks to Christ, even as the law had served a similar purpose among the Hebrews. But Clement did not neglect to add, as he could in all good conscience, that those Greeks who had seen God clearly through philosophy were ultimately indebted to Moses and the prophets, who were anterior to and more fully inspired than the wisest of the Greeks. Origen also, although he had been from early youth a devout Christian, regarded Greek philosophy so highly that he required his pupils to study it diligently. In his opinion a Christian could not attain to a truly worthy form of piety who did not think in the philosophical way.

By the middle of the third century ancient Christian doctrine had reached the highest eminence that it was ever to attain on the philosophical highway. Scholars had introduced into the church even more intellectualism than that institution was able to absorb. The transcendental Absolute of the philosophers was too remote a deity to function realistically in the rites of the church and thereby displace the saving Christ of popular faith, while the Logos Christology expounded by the learned theologians made Christ only a secondary god. Their offense against monotheism was not, however, the most serious difficulty, although their critics might urge it against them when a favorable opportunity offered. The fatal hurdle over which they stumbled was an implied diminution of the dignity attaching to Christ as the supreme object of worship in the church. The absolute validity of its sacraments was of greater moment to clerics and ordinary devotees than was the philosopher's metaphysical Absolute. Full satisfaction attached to the sacred ceremonies only when their efficacy was insured by a savior who was as completely deity as it was possible to imagine. The redeemer-Son had to be co-eternal and consubstantial with the Father. This was the fundamental difficulty underlying the theological controversy at the Council of Nicea, where again the will of the cult — as always — had its way.

LECTURE TWO

THE MARCH TO IMPERIALISM

Religious beliefs may be authenticated in either of two typical ways. They may derive their validity from the force of conviction with which they are held and advocated by individuals; or they may be given legal status by official action of a political or ecclesiastical establishment. In the latter event they are lifted out of the realm of persuasion or debate and take on the character of divine enactments. At an early date Christian thinking adopted this pattern. When voluntary beliefs were thus supplanted by prescribed dogmas, the enforcing institution acquired supreme authority. The church, as the symbol and agent of God's universal domin-ion, like the imperial Roman administration, assumed dic-tatorship over all the affairs of mankind.

During the second lap of its onward journey the Christian mind traveled far upon this imperial highway. Respect for traditional rites and doctrines, by which the faithful availed themselves of the salvation that Christ had made possible, gradually crystallized into reverence for the local church itself as a divine establishment. Later, the urge toward intellectual initiative on the part of individuals was so bitted and bridled that it added fresh increments of strength to the growing institution. Christian thinking became more effec-tively universalized by the bringing of the figure of the Supreme Deity into the center of the doctrinal picture.

Theology, used in the strict sense of the term, now took precedence over Christology; while the sufficiency of Christ's Saviorhood as mediated through the cult was preserved by his being made the equal of God in every respect. This task was too all-important to be left to the persuasive powers of individual thinkers; it was an obligation to be discharged by the corporate body of Christians. Henceforth the church was not only the channel through which Christ made salvation available for mankind; it was also the instrument chosen by Almighty God for making his rule dominant in the world.

I

The shift of emphasis from Christ to God and then to the organized church, while characteristic of the early Christian movement as a whole, was not equally prominent in all parts of Christendom. There was a line of cleavage between East and West more or less clearly discernible in the sphere of Christian doctrine long before these two sections of the Roman Empire became separate political units. The diverging trends were shaped by more fundamental facts of a social, cultural and psychological character.

In the East, where congregations had severally inherited the primitive emphasis on a mystical attachment to the Deity realized by means of rites celebrated in the local assemblies, need for a central administrative authority was not keenly felt. The desired unity was preserved in a consistent doctrine about the Savior-God. Thus Christology and theology were the primary concerns; ecclesiology in its unifying and universal aspects was at best only a secondary interest. The decisions of a council, enforced if need be by the imperial police, were the means trusted to establish and maintain the integrity and uniformity of Christianity. Furthermore, in the East the church's heritage from speculative philosophy remained too prominent ever to be completely supplanted by the ideal of submission to a single administrative head of Christendom. Even the decrees of councils and the commands of emperors could not prevent Eastern Christianity from breaking up into separate branches in accordance with the convictions of individuals and groups. An emperor might evict recalcitrant bishops from office but he could not prevent them and their followers from setting up independent churches. Nor was there any single bishopric whose antiquity and dignity were sufficient to establish its supremacy over all other episcopal sees. Under these circumstances Eastern Christian thinking did not take readily to the imperialistic type of ecclesiastical doctrine.

Conditions were different in the West. Apart from opinions taken over ready-made from the East, Western Christians in general showed only slight interest in or aptitude for speculative reasoning about either Christ or God. They were one with their Eastern brethren in affirming that God is the Supreme Creator and Christ is the all-sufficient Savior, both co-eternal and co-equal; but Westerners had surprisingly little to say for themselves on this subject. It concerned them only when they were called upon to defend current tradition against types of heretical thinking that emanated from the Orient.

In the West as in the East, membership in the worshiping community was valued highly and devotees not infrequently showed a fondness for mysticism. But in this respect also there was a difference. For the Western Christian worship was primarily an act of obedience. It might result in the divinization of the worshiper, if he were sensitive to that type of experience, but its more pervasive function was to insure divine help and approval. God required obedience. The Christian was devout in order to prove himself worthy of the divine benefactions in whatsoever form they might be conferred. Since God's dominion, like that of an emperor, was universal and his law, with its rewards for the obedient and its punishments for the offender, was everywhere the same, it was quite in order for Christian ideology in the West to stress the unity, universality and absolute supremacy of the divine government represented by the church. Hence ecclesiology readily became a subject of first importance. Until its status was fixed all other items of belief remained in jeopardy. Neither Christology, theology, soteriology, ethical theory, nor any other phase of Christian thinking could be authoritatively established so long as one's doctrine of the church was open to question. Christianity needed a valid ecclesiology by which everything else could be certified.

Western Christendom came naturally by the legal and governmental state of mind. Many forces had contributed to its making. Frequently the individuals chiefly responsible for giving direction to Christian thinking in the West had been trained for the legal profession or were teachers of Latin rhetoric, a discipline designed primarily to equip one for service in the law courts or in offices of state. Tertullian, Cyprian, Lactantius, Ambrose and even the versatile Augustine are conspicuous representatives of this class of person. In some instances Christian leaders had, at one time or another, actually held important positions under the secular authorities. This had been the case, for example, with Ambrose, Leo the Great and Gregory the Great. When the affairs of the church were directed by men familiar with the processes of Roman law and skilled in statecraft, the normal outcome was the growth of an ecclesiastical institution as juridically minded as the Roman political administration had ever been.

Years of conflict between Christianity and the Roman state also exerted a strong formative influence upon the development of the ecclesiastical consciousness. During the first two centuries the persecutions of Christians had been local and sporadic, hostility being directed against individual believers rather than the organized religious movement. But under Decius in 250 A.D. the struggle assumed new proportions, with the power of the imperial government definitely pitted against the church as a dangerous rival institution. A few years later under Valerian, and again under Diocletian in the first decade of the next century, the same policy was continued. The Christian church was held chiefly to blame for diverting the loyalties of the people from the protecting deities of the state to the foreign Christian divinities. The action most likely to correct this error seemed to be a vigorous effort to annihilate the church by crushing its hierarchy, destroying its houses of worship, confiscating its properties, burning its Scriptures and forbidding its sacred rites. When the institution had been wrecked its deluded adherents, so it was assumed, could be induced with a minimum of compulsion to resume allegiance to the tutelary gods of the state.

Under the pressure of conflict Christian thinkers sharpened their apologetic sword. They made it double-edged. They accepted without reserve the traditional Roman theory that stable government rested on divine sanctions, and from this major premise they made two deductions. First, they sought to cut the ground from under the old divinities by magnifying the disasters that had overtaken Roman society while it had been trusting in these ancient protectors. Mounting troubles only proved the frailty of the traditional gods. There was, therefore, but one valid alternative. The state ought to seek the aid of a more competent deity, and Christians proposed that their God be intrusted with this task. Galerius a few weeks before his death and Constantine at the outset of his political career granted the God of the Christians an opportunity to prove his competence in this sphere of action. The experiment proved so satisfactory to Constantine that in the course of time he came to depend chiefly upon this new source for the divine supports of his imperial regime.

The administrative mind was by its very nature more vitally concerned with the corporate integrity of a religious movement than with individual piety or the ceremonies of local congregations. A religion, like a state, needed above all else a smoothly operating organization to solidify individuals and groups into a consistent and effective unity.

From this point of view internal strife within the area of religious activities was as reprehensible as civil war within the state. This conviction prompted Constantine's efforts to allay the Donatist controversy in North Africa and the Arian dispute that he found raging in the East a decade later when that territory was added to his kingdom. He presupposed that centralized control was as practicable and essential for the health of the Christian commonwealth as it was for the political empire. Thus the patronage of the state became a powerful stimulus toward the development of an imperial ecclesiology.

As the course of events moved on new conditioning influences emerged. The Christian God had been installed in the guardianship of the Roman Empire, but time soon proved that he was unable or unwilling to stay the disruptive forces that had long been threatening the stability and permanence of the state. Either he was unequal to this task, or else the mechanisms thus far employed to mediate his assistance were defective. Christians, since they could accept only the second alternative, were now impelled to define more explicitly the nature of the church in respect to its administrative operations on the totalitarian level. The theoretical unity and dominance of Christianity had to be transformed into a practically workable reality within the actual operations of human society. In the East the problem was less acute because emperors, remaining in power, exercised control over ecclesiastical activities. But in the West, where the imperial government completely collapsed, the church was forced to assume full responsibility for representing God in the direction of the world's affairs. Only a thoroughly unified institution, conceived in terms of a corporate entity centrally controlled, could function adequately in this situation.

The consequent effort to define more precisely the nature and validity of the church in its new role was further conditioned by the geographical distribution of Western Christianity. At first there had been two principal territories, Italy and North Africa, in which the new religion gained its firmest footing. While the relations between these two sections of Christendom were in the main friendly, each enjoyed a prestige of its own and displayed certain distinctive traits that might have proved embarrassing to later ecclesiologists had they ultimately been compelled to decide in favor of the one or the other when it came to a question of locating the seat of supreme authority. But this prospective difficulty was removed by political events over which theologians had no control. The triumph of the Vandals in the fifth century and conquest by the Mohammedans in the seventh wiped the church off the North African map. The Italian church alone remained pre-eminent in the West. In Spain and Gaul, it is true, Christianity survived, but in neither territory was its prestige sufficient to constitute a serious obstacle to the growing ascendency of the Italian church, particularly in Rome. Ancient Christian tradition and the political renown of the eternal city combined to give the bishop of Rome every advantage when the problem of locating the residence of Christianity's imperial ruler in the West became a vital issue.

The ecclesiastical mind of that day was shaped by still another influence of fundamental importance, although it is not so readily definable. It was not unlike a phenomenon that we shall meet with again when we come to the twentieth century. It was a sort of popular drift, an undercurrent of sentiment, that shook confidence in the ability of man as philosopher and moralist to attain unto ultimate truth and virtue, however sincere and strenuous the efforts of individuals and specific groups might be. Just as the different philosophical schools in the Roman Empire were relaxing their trust in personal intellectual initiative in favor of reliance upon external authorities, so people in general were prone to seek assurances for their well-being in some mechanism of control lying outside of and beyond the range of their immediate individual responsibility. Man bowed in hopeless submission — not voluntarily but of necessity — to a higher will. This overruling power might be a divine emperor, or the decrees of destiny read from the stars, or the arbitrary operations of blind fate, or any other inscrutable cosmic force. To work out one's own salvation was thought to be a futile endeavor. A sense of frustration became the highest of virtues. It was an age conspicuously marked by " failure of nerve."

The religious mind never could, and never does, come to rest in mere frustration. This is only a preparation for the acceptance of a certain type of theological deduction. In the ancient world release from this defeatist obsession was found in religious authoritarianism, either pagan or Christian. But in this sphere Christianity easily outstripped its competitors. The claims it had already made for its Savior, its Scriptures, its sacraments and its God had only to be extended to its unified institution in order to establish completely its supremacy in a world where all the older sureties were rapidly crumbling. This state of affairs became especially acute in the West with the collapse of the imperial government and the conquest of the territory by the barbarian settlers. Christian doctrines, if they were to have vital meaning for people, had to be shaped in accordance with the state of mind imposed upon that world by the realistic conditions of contemporary life.

II

In the early stages of its journey along the imperial highway the Christian mind moved at varying rates of speed past a great variety of scenery, and often in doubt about the best course to pursue. Some thinkers were alert and clearvisioned. Others were awkward or near-sighted, slow to extract themselves from difficult situations and hesitant in taking advantage of opportunities for progress. Even the most competent guides were sometimes baffled by the low visibility of the atmosphere or the perplexing curvature of the roads. Frequently uncertain as to their destination, they could not advance with purposeful assurance. In general, their activities seem to have been inspired by the wish to escape the inconveniences of an immediate situation rather than by any controlling determination to reach a clearly envisaged goal.

Intellectual attainments, in the strict sense of the term,

were rarely or never the chief objective of these Christian leaders. Philosophical speculation was not native to the Western mind as it was to that of the East. Neither metaphysical questions nor the refinements of logic had any strong attraction for Western thinkers. Their dominating interests were practical and ethical. Right opinion and proper conduct were supremely important to them, but the test of rectitude in thought and action was conformity to ancient tradition and the maintenance of orderly government in the church. With this as their fundamental principle, the framers of Christian doctrine worked their way through successive crises. We shall attempt a brief survey of the main issues that were forced upon their attention.

North Africa and Gaul, rather than Italy, furnished Western Christendom its first generation of doctrinal leaders. Irenaeus, Tertullian and Cyprian were its brightest luminaries. Justin Martyr had, indeed, conducted a Christian school in Rome, but his heritage and chief theological concerns were prevailingly Eastern in type. Tertullian and Cyprian were genuinely Western in training and sentiment; while Irenaeus, although a man of the East and much indebted to the ideas of Justin Martyr, thoroughly identified himself with the interests of Western Christianity as viewed from the situation in southern Gaul, where first as a presbyter and then as a bishop he spent the last quarter century of his life.

The contribution of Irenaeus to the evolution of Christian doctrine at the close of the second century still remains a conspicuous landmark on the Western highway. His was not a great creative mind, and the motive that prompted him to theologize was the immediate necessity of resisting Gnostic propaganda that now menaced the unity of the church even in the West. He refuted heresy from the point of view of the practical churchman. Instead of pursuing the methods of an orthodox Christian philosopher like Clement of Alexandria, who reasoned that traditional Christian doctrine embodied the true knowledge (*gnosis*) and that even the wisdom of the Greeks had been in reality a preparation for faith in Christ, Irenaeus stressed the authority of Christian tradition, the efficacy of the sacred rites, the dependability of canonized books and the validity of the Catholic church.

Irenaeus accepted the Gnostics' pessimistic estimate of man's physical being, not because matter in and of itself was hopelessly evil, as the Gnostics alleged, but because Adam had disobeyed God and hence all of Adam's descendents suffered the taint of corruption. Thus humanity, having fallen under the control of Satan, had lost its divine title to immortality. The consequences of this disobedience could be averted only through membership in the church. By means of his famous doctrine of recapitulation Irenaeus provided redemption for both the body and the soul of man. Christ who was fully God had also become truly man, the second Adam, who summed up in his career, without repeating the mistake of the first Adam, the life of ideal humanity — a humanity which before Adam's fall had been divine in its nature and immortal both as flesh and as spirit. In Christ humanity, again becoming deified, had been restored to its original God-status. It was the peculiar function of the church to mediate to believers the re-deification that Christ had made possible. This ontological mysticism was for Irenaeus the essence of true Christianity, in contrast with the Gnostic emphasis on salvation through epistemological mysticism.

At first sight Irenaeus' notion of salvation through the deification of one's being might seem to be only a replica of Pauline thinking. Undoubtedly this mystical emphasis was carried over from Asia Minor where Irenaeus had received his early training in Christianity, but it was regularized and subordinated to the ecclesiastical institution in a way that certainly would have been distasteful to Paul. While the value of the cultus was stressed in truly Eastern fashion, Irenaeus passed very lightly over the theistic, Christological and cosmological problems that long engrossed the attention of leading theologians in the East. His program called primarily for obedience, not for philosophical or logical justification of doctrine. Christ's obedience to God and man's obedience to the church constituted the foundations on which the scheme of salvation rested, just as Adam's disobedience had occasioned the calamity that made a program of redemption necessary. By thus making legalistic imagery the basis of his thinking, Irenaeus proved himself to be a genuine exponent of the Western temper.

In meeting the crisis raised by the Gnostics, Irenaeus laid the foundations on which the entire system of Western ecclesiastical doctrine was reared. Fallen humanity, in both its fleshly and its spiritual aspects, was transformed into divine being through the sacraments. On entering the church one received "the baptism of regeneration unto God." Ceasing to be merely human, one became a participant in eternal and unalterable deity. Repeated observance of the eucharist augmented the process which rendered the physical body incorruptible and thus insured resurrection unto eternal life. This deification was progressive: " We are not made gods at the outset, but at first man, then at length gods." God, who created the first man in the image of the divine, had now provided a plan by which fallen men could be restored to their original God-likeness.

God, whom the ancient Scriptures of the church revealed, and not merely Christ as the Gnostics alleged, was for Irenaeus the real Savior. Yet Irenaeus was enough of a philosopher to concede that ultimate deity ought to be described in terms of transcendence, as uncreated, immaterial, invisible and unapproachable by finite creatures. Therefore Christ, the Logos, the Son of God, needed to intervene. But Irenaeus could not so far follow Justin Martyr, whose doctrine of the Logos he accepted, as to call Christ a " second " God; for if Christ were not very God himself the sacraments performed in his name would not necessarily insure the full deification of the worshiper. Hence Irenaeus explicitly affirmed that " the Father is Lord and the Son is Lord, the Father is God and the Son is God, for that which is begotten of God is God."

Gnostic depreciation of the Old Testament also seemed to Irenaeus an outright sin against the Holy Spirit, whose testimony authenticated not only the ancient Scriptures but also the beliefs and practices of the later church. The Spirit had enabled the prophets to forecast unerringly events leading up to Christ's advent. This divine presence was also resident in the incarnate Christ. Christ and the Spirit were hardly distinguishable in much of Irenaeus' language. In the apostles and their successors the same power remained active, giving to the church a divine quality by virtue of which it could, one might say, itself beget sons of God. The metaphysical issues involved in this imagery did not trouble Irenaeus. He was convinced that within the church one found in operation the plenitude of the Godhead. Any divine guidance that Gnostics or Marcionites or Montanists might claim for themselves outside of an orthodox communion was only an empty shadow. The Spirit and the church mutually accredited each other: " Where the church is there is the Spirit of God, and where the Spirit of God is there is the church." Assuming that the truth preached by the true church is everywhere and always the same, Irenaeus concluded that those who cut themselves off from this Spirit-inspired fellowship " defrauded themselves of life through their perverse opinions and infamous behavior."

While Irenaeus did not develop his doctrine of the church in systematic detail, he laid solid foundations for the superstructure and determined the main features of the building that his successors were to erect. The church was essentially a sacramental institution beyond whose pale there could be no salvation. It was the one establishment set up by God to implement his perfect dispensation of grace and truth. The revelation given in the Old Testament, the activities of

Christ, the teaching of the apostles, the present operations of the Spirit of God, the writing and preservation of just four canonical Gospels, and the divinely established episcopal form of government had all been designed to serve this end. Christian teaching — the " rule of faith " — rested on the three great pillars of apostolic preaching about God, Christ and the Holy Spirit. Unity and consistency of doctrine no longer depended upon rationally justified conclusions arrived at by individual theologians, but upon the postulate of universal institutional regularity. Certainty was established by means of a faithful succession of leaders, tracing from Christ through apostles and presbyters to bishops. They had thus received the " sure gift of truth in accordance with the Father's good pleasure," a fact sadly ignored by heretics and schismatics.

That bishops might disagree among themselves was for Irenaeus an improbable contingency. Since divine truth by its very nature must be indivisible and self-consistent, and is the precious treasure which " the church in all the world hands on to its children," all true bishops in every age necessarily spoke with one voice. On this hypothesis no single church was sovereign in its own right, not even that of Rome, but the latter enjoyed unique dignity, having been " founded and organized by the two most illustrious apostles, Peter and Paul." Should a crisis arise, the prestige of the Roman episcopate would make it the proper source of final appeal. Irenaeus has been appropriately called the father of Catholic dogma. He laid the foundations of an ecclesiology excellently designed to preserve the Christian movement from disintegration under the impact of those destructive forces that were beating upon it in western Europe at the close of the second century.

III

In North Africa, where Tertullian at the opening of the third century and Cyprian fifty years later directed the course of Christian doctrine, there was a similar type of compulsive motivation for thinking. These leaders set themselves to resist the menace of growing irregularities that threatened the solidarity of the Christian religion. Generally speaking, one may specify three chief causes of anxiety. First, there was the increasing hostility of the Roman political authorities who perceived ever more clearly that the church as a developing institution was becoming virtually a rival state within the Empire. Secondly, there was the multiplication of heretics and sectaries whose activities tended further to disrupt the ideal unity of Christendom. And thirdly, among church members themselves there was a marked decline of uniformity in moral and religious conduct inevitably resulting from growth in numbers and the varied relations amid which Christians strove to maintain their physical existence within a non-Christian social environment.

Both Tertullian and Cyprian, being men of an eminently legal cast of mind, thought naturally in terms of juristic imagery. Since the church was an institution for implementing the law of God, it was thereby empowered to withstand the persecutor and to impose upon its members both a law of faith and a law of discipline. In characteristic Roman fashion religion was made essentially a matter of contract between deity and mankind. It presupposed the absolute sovereignty of God and the unquestioning obedience of man. These sign-posts indicated clearly the highway to be further explored by Christian thinkers, who needed to frame a doctrine regarding the relation between church and state that would render the supremacy of the Christian Deity a tenable opinion even at a time when its validity seemed to be denied by the unrestrained hostility of the Roman authorities. And if the fundamental virtue of absolute obedience to God was to be realized by members of the Christian society, the functions of the church as an instrument for enforcing God's will among men needed to be more specifically defined.

Tertullian and Cyprian were both sufficiently Roman in their sentiments and Stoic in their philosophy of life to place a rather high estimate upon the benefits accruing to society from the efficiency of the imperial government and to see in the natural order the operations of a divine providence. They knew that all was not well with their world, but Christians no less than Stoics possessed their souls in patience. For the moment God permitted the Roman state to exist, wicked though many of its operations were in consequence of the invasion of society by demons who were responsible for idolatry, moral degeneration and hostility to Christianity. In the meantime, however, the Kingdom of God, which was the church in its ideal solidarity, had made its initial appearance upon the scene. Ultimately it would triumph, neither by absorbing nor by conquering the state, but by God's

sudden intervention to usher in the day of judgment fore-
told by the prophets. The Jewish-Christian hope of the
millennial age had not faded completely from the distant
horizon, nor had the statesmen of the church as yet envisaged
the day when emperors would kneel at the altar to receive
the blessing of a Christian bishop. For the moment the
church was content to avail itself of the advantages offered
by a stable political administration without which, as Tertullian conceded, the church would find itself in sore straits.

The church was nevertheless an institution superior to the
state and could, in the opinion of Tertullian, have successfully withstood its persecutors had not Christian teaching
denied the propriety of violent resistance. He vigorously
affirmed the right of the church to be recognized as a corporate body in Roman law, but even if not so recognized it was
a divine corporation with its own assemblies, times and
places of meeting, official orders and magistrates, all subject
to the imperial authority of God. The church was in reality
a state since all its members, although citizens of a heavenly
kingdom, existed on earth as a corporate entity possessing a
specific religious belief, a unity of discipline and a common
bond of hope. This truly divine institution, by establishing
itself in the present world, was really the power that held
imperial society together. The church prayed for all governmental officials and particularly for emperors, not because
the Caesar was a deity but because he was the person to
whom the Supreme God had temporarily intrusted chief
responsibility for political affairs.

Moreover, Christians, who were now to be found in all

the walks of life not excluding even the army, had injected a new increment of divine energy into the Roman Empire. Tertullian refused outright to allow that Rome's glory had been a gift from the ancient gods. But in the same breath, repeating the religious theory on which this claim was based, he declared that the traditional God of the Christians was the Lord of kingdoms. Had the Jews not sinned against him, and finally against Christ, their nation, we are told, would never have been conquered by the Romans. Now the Romans were making a similar mistake by refusing worship to the Supreme God " to whom," says Tertullian, " whether we will or not we all belong."

It was a common disposition, said Tertullian, to concede sovereignty to one divine power and to allocate his functions to many subordinates. Tertullian had in mind at the moment the religious and political philosophy of his non-Christian contemporaries, but he might have used this language with entire propriety to epitomize his Christian thinking. The absolute sovereignty of God was its major premise. This postulate was not supported by any metaphysical or philosophical justification; it seemed to Tertullian axiomatic. It was primarily a governmental conception stressing the authority and majesty of a personal ruler, fear of whom constituted the basis of all virtue and whose commands were to be obeyed not because they were thought to be good but because they were divine enactments. God was the supreme monarch whose imperial decrees were inviolable.

Man's disobedience to God had brought about the unhappy situation which it was Christianity's mission to correct. Disobedience was an act of the human will, guilt was its consequence, and unless forgiveness was obtained and obedience restored, eternal punishment would be its reward. Unlike Irenaeus, Tertullian showed no traces of Eastern mysticism in his thinking. Adam's fall had not meant the corruption of a human nature that now needed re-deification; rather, Adam had incurred a debt of disobedience inherited and repeated by his descendents. This violation of the divine legislation placed mankind in the position of the guilty criminal in the law court of the sovereign God. The entire human race stood condemned in the sight of an avenging Deity, and guilt involved sure punishment unless pardon was granted. God had willed that forgiveness might be obtained if certain conditions were fulfilled. Immunity could be " purchased by the payment of repentance " and a strenuous display of strict obedience. By repentance " God is appeased " and by the assiduous practices of penitence one may " expunge eternal punishment."

Since God had decreed that the church is the only instrument for mediating salvation, it was of primary importance to establish the ecclesiastical institution on a sure foundation in Christian thinking. Ecclesiology was the cardinal item in Christian doctrine. The church's " rule of faith " had the validity of a divine imperial decree. Its traditions were sacred and infallible. Its sacraments were administered by magisterial officials, subordinates of a sovereign God, who assigned them their specific duties. The clergy were a distinct class apart from the laity — a differentiation first made by Tertullian and further stressed by Cyprian. Clerical acts were sacramental operations that in time were to become sacred in their own right irrespective of the personal character of the minister, just as the validity of Roman law was superior to the magistrate by whom it was administered. Heretics and schismatics, by the very fact of their apostasy from the church, deprived themselves of all rights before God. You did not debate questions with a heretic; you simply anathematized him. He had committed the heinous sin of disobedience. Being guilty of high treason against God, he deserved the penalty of death. Truth, both practically and intellectually, was guaranteed by the authority of the church.

How to make the authority of the church effectively operative was as yet the great unsolved problem. The laity were not always amenable to discipline and even the clergy were often contentious. Ultimately Tertullian grew so restless under the failure of the Catholic church to enforce its discipline that he was thrown into the arms of Montanism, while Cyprian spent his best energies in the effort to remedy the chaotic state of moral and ecclesiastical affairs in North Africa. The laxity of the laity, especially in time of persecution, the arrogance of rival clerics, the continuance of heresy and schism, and other internal disorders in the Christian society combined to impress upon Cyprian the necessity of defining more explicitly the means by which the ideal unity of the church could be made really effective. The result was his most significant contribution to Christian doctrine — his interpretation of episcopacy.

Episcopal authority was accepted by Tertullian and Cyp-

rian, as it had been by Irenaeus. Christ had appointed
apostles, they in turn had founded the first episcopal sees,
and the successions of bishops had guarded the purity of the
Christian tradition. Thus episcopal teaching was a unity
because it was the continuing voice of divine revelation.
Theoretically, dissonance was impossible; but in reality the
impossible was happening with embarrassing frequency.
Therefore Cyprian undertook to formulate and justify a plan
by which harmony could be secured in the episcopal chorus.
He adopted for this purpose a procedure modeled after the
municipal and provincial conciliar system long established
as a feature of the political administration. On occasion the
church had already resorted to synods of bishops to settle
certain local disputes. But heretofore these assemblies were
only voluntary gatherings of bishops whose authority resided in the fact that they held office because chosen by their
respective congregations and approved by at least three
neighboring bishops. By right of appointment they belonged in the apostolic succession, but in joint assembly they
were not united by any superior principle of solidarity. Apparently no one had yet supposed that Christ had authorized
councils.

Cyprian, at a council of North African bishops in the year
251, advanced the notion that the unity of the church centered in the collective episcopate declaring its will with one
voice through an ecclesiastical synod. The theory was justified by reference to Christ's choice of all the apostles, whom
he endowed equally with authority. He had mentioned
Peter first, not because Peter received a unique endowment,

but simply to indicate the unity in which the episcopal authority began and must be perpetuated. There was just one church throughout the world although divided by Christ into many members, and likewise there was but one episcopate represented by a harmonious multitude of bishops. Their first duty was to hold fast and confirm this unity by participating individually in the will of the whole.

This was a very significant administrative concept. It provided a concrete instrument for enforcing the ideal unity of Christendom by giving to an episcopal assembly a dignity transcending that of any individual bishop. A council possessed divine authority conferred upon it by Christ. One must avoid in this connection the mistake of assuming the presence of any notion of representative government. Bishops were not delegates from their respective congregations authorized to voice the will of their several churches. Authority came from above mediated by the Spirit speaking for Christ, the imperial head of the church. The principle of unity resided in the assumption that it was impossible for the divine will ever to be self-contradictory or to sponsor discordant opinions. But the scheme suffered from a serious limitation. In the event of a divided assembly, who was empowered to cast the deciding vote? And who would suppress recalcitrant minorities? A similar difficulty plagues all of our modern attempts to construct a machinery for uniting Christendom. Voluntary co-operation is one thing while administrative compulsion is quite another. In Cyprian's day voluntarism was an untenable proposition; his thinking demanded a supreme power acting, or capable of acting, to eliminate all dissidents. Pushed to its logical conclusion, the conception required for its effective operation either a Christian prince to enforce the decisions of a council, or a bishop of bishops to transcend its authority. Cyprian's program provided for neither of these earthly potentates.

In the next century, when Constantine legalized Christianity and his successors made it the official religion of their kingdom, Christian thinking moved more easily along the imperial highway. The toilsome ascent of earlier days now threatened to become a headlong plunge down grade into a morass of political entanglements. Grateful for the cessation of persecutions and appreciative of an Emperor's support, theologians generally paid excessive deference to the whims and prejudices of princes. These rulers were ready to support by force if necessary the unity of Christendom, while at the same time they practiced a totalitarian philosophy that virtually subordinated the church to the state. Emperors called or sanctioned Christian assemblies, more or less closely supervised their procedures, and tacitly or openly reserved the right to accept or reject synodical and conciliar decisions. These conditions did not encourage a vigorous type of independent Christian thinking.

Nevertheless it is a fact that the most notable theological dispute in the ancient church, the Arian controversy, fell in this period. But the importance of the famous Council of Nicea for the development of Christian doctrine was quite out of proportion to the attention it has attracted. It dealt with only one crucial item of belief, the relation between the Father and the Son in the Godhead, and made no new contribution to thinking even on that subject. Devout ecclesiastics from Irenaeus to Athanasius, whose fundamental concern had been with the soteriological significance of Christ mediated through the sacraments of the church, had already established the wide popularity of belief in the co-eternity and consubstantiality of the Father and the Son. To all of this the Council of Nicea added essentially nothing except official definition and confirmation. But in that fact lay its fundamental significance. For the first time in history ecclesiastical legislation transcended both ancient tradition and individual apprehension of truth as norms for justifying the beliefs of Christians. Faith became dogma; an official creed asserted lordship over conscience and intellect. This was a triumph of the imperialistic temper, a victory for the Western spirit, the marks of which still remain indelibly stamped upon much of our Christian thinking even to the present day.

IV

By the close of the fourth century the will of emperors showed unmistakable signs of losing its control over the Western world. The task of holding society together and providing a unifying interpretation of life's meaning devolved increasingly upon churchmen. With the disintegration of political power the enfeebled hand of government was no longer able to impose one form of dogma or one type of ecclesiastical practice upon a dissolving Empire. Conflicting interests and opinions, advantaged by the weakening of secular authority, reasserted themselves with new vigor.

Leaders of the church were forced to assume more immediate responsibility for directing and unifying the thinking of the age. Ambrose and Augustine will illustrate sufficiently for our present purpose the course along which Christian doctrine now moved.

The Nicene controversy had issued in the establishment of two branches of Christendom, the Catholic and the Arian, each of which from time to time enjoyed the approval of the state. The barbarian settlers within the Empire were in the main attached to the Arian churches, thanks to the missionary labors of Ulfilas who had been consecrated at Constantinople Bishop of the Goths in the year 348 when Arianism was in favor at the Eastern capital. Even in the West Arianism under imperial patronage had gained wide influence. Ambrose's predecessor in the episcopal see of Milan had been an outspoken Arian who held office for twenty years despite the vigorous efforts of the Catholic Bishop of Poitiers to oust this " angel of Satan, enemy of Christ, desperate devastator, denier of the faith." Christian disunion still seemed to be an incurable malady, notwithstanding the general acceptance of the doctrine of a state church. No means had yet been advanced for controlling the ecclesiastical affiliation of princes. This was one of the crucial issues to which Ambrose devoted much thought and energy.

The principal weapon used by Ambrose was his power of persuasion, backed by his inherited attachment to Catholicism, his personal strength of mind and character, and his administrative experience as a statesman before episcopal responsibilities were suddenly thrust upon him in the year

373. Shortly afterwards the joint emperors, Valentinian I and Valens, the one having tolerated and the other ardently espoused Arianism, were removed by death. Their successors, with whom Ambrose was frequently brought into contact since Milan was now the imperial residence in the West, lent their support to the Catholic branch of Christendom. But apparently Ambrose realized the need for the church to assert its superiority to the state, or even to the decision of a council sponsored by an unorthodox emperor. The trend of previous Christian thinking, by which church and state had been brought together, was not reversed, but the way was paved for a further expansion of episcopal power.

The doctrine of the supremacy of the church over the state emerged clearly upon the horizon of Ambrose's thinking. He was a diligent student of the Eastern theologians, under whose influence he conceived the church to be a divinely established sacramental institution. But his stress on man's obedience to the rites of the church as a means of escape from guilt and a guarantee of heavenly bliss was thoroughly Western in spirit. And he anticipated Augustine in so emphasizing the imperial autonomy and autocracy of God as to make prevenient grace the indispensable condition of man's ability to turn from evil and obtain salvation. The acceptance of orthodox doctrine, for Ambrose the essence of faith, was followed by the cleansing rite of baptism. This sacrament cancelled one's past sins. As in the case of the flood, " water is that in which the flesh is purged to wash away every sin of the flesh." One thus regenerated received

an anointing " with spiritual grace unto the kingdom of
God." Then followed the rite of foot-washing " that heredi-
tary sins may be removed, our own sins having been removed by baptism." Now clad in a white robe the initiates
whose guilt had been " sunk in the waters " of baptism
hastened to the altar of Christ to partake of the eucharist.
When the priest repeated Christ's words of institution, the
bread and the wine became his actual body and blood, the
very " substance of eternal life." The entire procedure represented a divinely ordained operation of supernatural grace.
Since this was mediated only through the church, it transcended all other organizations in human society not excluding even the imperial Roman government.

Ambrose strove continually to bend emperors to his will
in all matters involving morality, belief and ecclesiastical
procedure. When they hesitated or refused to obey the commands of God uttered by the bishop, he in turn refused to
perform the sacraments, without which the immortal soul
of man was doomed to eternal torment. Now that the
church had attained to this dominance over the minds of
people generally, even princes dared not resist the powerful
pressure of heaven. Yet Ambrose, cautiously or politely, affirmed that it was only in the sphere of faith that " bishops
are wont to pass judgment on Christian emperors, not emperors on bishops." But evidently faith was taken to embrace a wide range of temporal affairs including private and
public morality, the abolition of pagan religious rites, the
suppression of heresies, the granting of immunities to the
orthodox clergy, and the exclusive legalization of the Catho-

lic church throughout the emperor's domains. So successful had Ambrose been in promulgating his doctrine of the church that Theodosius, the last ruler of the undivided Roman Empire, may in a very real sense be called a servant of the church. Ambrose's funeral oration in honor of the deceased prince was not all empty rhetoric. Alluding to the nail from the cross that Helena, the mother of Constantine, was said to have inserted in his crown, Ambrose saw the prophecy of a hope that had now become a reality. Helena's act had not been one of insolence but of true piety in that the cross of Christ had thus been placed above the head of princes. Although they ruled over the vast Roman Empire they had been changed from persecutors into heralds of the church.

It remained for Augustine to pursue to its logical conclusion the idea of the church as a supernatural *imperium*. This is not the place to enter upon a detailed account of the rich and varied elements involved in the elaborate theological system of the famous African. But the one persistent quest that dominated all of his efforts was to discover and then to defend the reliable source of authority wherein his mind and his heart could come to rest.

From his Christian upbringing Augustine had inherited the notion that knowledge of God is the supremely desirable attainment. Whence was this knowledge to be obtained? Catholic Christianity derived it from the divinely authorized ecclesiastical institution and its inspired canonical writings, but that procedure did not appeal to the youthful Augustine. His alert mind rebelled against the subordination of his personality to the authority of the institution, and his aesthetic literary tastes were offended by the crude Latin in which the Scriptures were current in North Africa. He looked elsewhere for a more rational and cultural type of individual satisfaction.

At the outset it was not the Catholic communion but the fellowship of the Manichean branch of the Christian church that seemed to Augustine to offer him the help he needed. Its theologians applied rational tests to the ancient Scriptures and made faith subject to the dictates of logic, while at the same time they claimed to restore the original and true form of Christianity. For a decade Augustine sought light from this source. But as his intellectualism became more mature he grew increasingly distrustful of Manichean rationalism. It lacked the religious depth that his soul craved. Especially was he dissatisfied with what seemed to him to be a totally inadequate solution of the problem of evil. Manichean teachers could tell him how to act in order to escape evil but they could not give him a reasonable explanation of its cause. Their pragmatism was too shallow to meet the demands of his inquisitive mind. He said they gave him only an empty cup when he asked for a draught of " truth."

First at Carthage and later at Rome and Milan new influences impinged upon Augustine. All the while he continued to travel the lonely road of the philosophical seeker after truth. During his residence in Rome he fell temporarily under the spell of the skeptical Academics. He concluded that perhaps after all ultimate knowledge might be unattainable. The physical senses often deceived one, logic might err for lack of adequate data, and even moral standards might not be absolutely determinable. During this period of uncertainty his attention was drawn to Plotinus, founder of Neoplatonism, whose writings had recently been rendered into Latin by Victorinus, at this time the most prominent rhetorician in Rome. A new world of thought was now opened up to Augustine's restless spirit. Following the lead of Plotinus, he found escape from bondage to critical observation of data and the limitations of cold logic. Neoplatonic mysticism gave him access to the super-sensible reality of pure Being, the ultimate Good, the supreme Unity, whose existence was authentically attested within the innermost emotions of the responsive soul. Thus dawned upon Augustine the major premise on which all of his subsequent Christian thinking was based. God is all in all — almighty will, only true being, source of all good, fountain of all life and truth, all-ruling providence, determiner of man's destines and supreme sovereign over all temporal and eternal affairs.

Belief in the divine sovereignty was so pre-eminent in Augustine's thinking that at first Christology and ecclesiology scarcely attracted his attention. While Neoplatonism had opened for him the mystical highway to God, Augustine identified this new-found divine being with the Christian Deity, knowledge of whom was revealed in the Scriptures and whose grace was mediated to mankind through the rites of the church. The allegorical interpretation exemplified in the preaching of Ambrose, and the majestic ceremonies of the worship at Milan evidently laid to rest Augustine's former scruples regarding the rational and aesthetic shortcomings of the Catholicism that he had known in his youth. He bowed to the authority of Catholic tradition and ritual without exercising his mind especially about these matters. He was bent upon cultivating a life of personal piety and meditation in the company of a few like-minded friends who retired with him to his native Tagaste in North Africa to devote their time to study and writing. Had not unforeseen circumstances intervened, compelling him to assume the active responsibilities of an ecclesiastical statesman during the last thirty-five years of his life, he might have become a Western Origen pursuing the individualistic way of the Christian philosopher's quest for truth. In that event he, like Origen, might have failed to attain to sainthood. Elements in his thinking that proved unappropriable by the institution might easily have brought his name and fame into disrepute in the later church and thus have robbed him of his distinction as the most conspicuous beacon on the highway of Western Christian doctrine.

In the year 395 Augustine, quite against his inclinations, was made bishop of the Catholic church at Hippo Regius in North Africa where he continued in active service until his death in 430. This was a fateful period in the history of the West. In the same year that Augustine entered upon his episcopal duties the death of Theodosius brought to an end the united Roman Empire. Almost immediately the rising tide of migration from across the Rhine and the Danube spread unhindered into Italy, Gaul, Spain and North Africa. Dissolution bordering on chaos threatened the older social order that had been maintained by the Roman government. Even so firmly established an institution as the Catholic church was shaken to its very foundations.

The Arian church was patronized by barbarian princes. The Donatist church, that had been in existence for more than a century, remained unsuppressed. The Manichean church continued its activities. The new Christian movement of the Pelagians arose and spread widely throughout the West. And surviving paganism threatened to become aggressive as it pointed the finger of scorn at the Christians who for a hundred years had been proclaiming that their God was the one divine ruler able to give prosperity and peace to the world. Almost a century had passed since Constantine legalized Christianity, and now the Goths under Alaric had actually captured and plundered Rome, the very citadel of political and ecclesiastical prestige.

Augustine, confident that the Catholic church was the sole organ of God's sovereignty on earth, now found himself faced with the tremendous task of rephrasing Christian doctrine to meet one of the most crucial situations in which a theologian has ever been placed. His fundamental belief in the all-sufficiency of God was only enhanced by the evident failure of men to direct their affairs to a successful issue. A similar disillusionment experienced by post-war theologians at the present time has resulted in reviving certain features stressed by Augustine in his formulation of fifth century Christian doctrine. It seemed sheer folly for man to arrogate to himself any power or responsibility for effecting his own or the world's salvation. God was almighty while man was utterly impotent. But Augustine had unlimited confidence in the Catholic church as the instrument used by God to realize his inscrutable purposes. A bishop, charged with the responsibility of defending the authority and integrity of his institution, could hardly have thought otherwise. Therefore his primary duty now was to elaborate a consistent and comprehensive doctrine of the church, an adequate ecclesiology — a theme that had previously been of slight if any concern to Augustine.

Remaining true to his fundamental Neoplatonic postulate that God is the only true, unchangeable and absolute being, whose will is supreme and determinative for all things, Augustine held the church to be a completely divine and in no sense a human establishment. Thus he accepted and zealously defended its traditional claims to apostolic origin, ideal unity, sacramental validity, universal authority and divine sovereignty on earth. Since it possessed a system of revealed truth to be imposed upon the minds of men, the church was the only agency that could mediate God's grace and salvation to helpless humanity. This hypothesis not only equipped the bishop to deal summarily with all foes of the Catholic church but it set the pattern into which he fitted the various details of his more completely developed theological system.

Although Augustine taught that the Catholic church was infallible and supreme, the circumstances of his day did not permit a definition of the concrete means by which its authority was to be enforced. No single episcopal see had as yet attained the necessary prestige to justify its dominance over all others. The decisions of councils, whether local or ecumenical, had been too variant and inconclusive to establish their indubitable finality. And Christian princes had often fallen far short of their duty in supporting Catholic dogma. If bishops, councils and Christian rulers might err, then how could the supremacy of the church be established? From this dilemma Augustine found a way of escape in his theory of the perfection of the invisible church, of which the visible one was as yet only the incomplete manifestation. In its current state of visibility it was indeed the Kingdom of God on earth, and hence the true church, although not at the moment regnant over all mundane affairs. Its gradual but inevitable triumph required time — in fact, a thousand years beginning with the days when Jesus, appearing upon earth, had begun to invade the devil's domains. The progress of the church toward ultimate victory was envisaged on a grand scale in Augustine's monumental treatise on the *City of God*.

Society outside of the Kingdom of God was termed by Augustine the " earthly city " in contrast with the heavenly " City of God." In respect to visibility the two estates existed together on the terrestrial plane, the Catholic church representing the latter and all political establishments, the Roman government in particular, representing the former. Constitutionally the two entities were utterly foreign to each other, but in the sphere of immediate action they were intimately related and not necessarily antagonistic. Augustine says explicitly: " The earthly city, which does not live by faith, seeks an earthly peace and the end it professes in the well-ordered concord of civic obedience and rule is the combination of men's wills to attain the things that are helpful to this life. . . . Even the heavenly city therefore, while in its state of pilgrimage, avails itself of the peace of earth and, so far as it can without injuring faith and godliness, desires and maintains a common agreement among men regarding the acquisition of the necessities of life and makes this earthly peace bear upon the peace of heaven. For this alone can be truly called and esteemed the peace of reasonable creatures, consisting as it does in the perfectly ordered and harmonious enjoyment of God and of one another in God " (*De civitate dei,* XIX, 17). In other words, it was the high privilege of the state to serve the purposes of the church. Opposing the Donatists, who now contended for the complete separation of church and state, Augustine affirmed that it was the duty of the government to suppress, by force if necessary, all heretics. The Catholic church, since it was the sole organ of the almighty will of God on earth, was entitled to impose its will upon all governments.

One may note in passing that the doctrine of an imperial church was not something arbitrarily foisted upon the ancient world. The theory of Petrine supremacy proved to be a convenient justification for the leadership that Roman bishops were ultimately enabled by circumstances to assume, and aggressive individuals were quite ready to cite this theory to augment their prestige. But the foundations on which this doctrinal superstructure rested have to be sought in the long process of antecedent historical events and conditions that placed the Roman church in the strategic and responsible situation where it found itself in the fifth century under the competent direction of Leo the Great and Gelasius the First. Just how much was involved in its responsibility might still be vague at certain points. But no one seriously questioned the desirability of ecclesiastical control over all human affairs or thought God's help obtainable otherwise than through the church. As God was one and supreme, so the church was unitary and universal in its power.

LECTURE THREE

TRAMPING OLD TRAILS

For a thousand years after the death of Augustine the Catholic establishment continued to tighten its grip on the Western world. Greek intellectualism was completely supplanted by Latin legalism; while canon law, unified and enlarged, acquired a dignity transcending that of civil law, whether of the new kingdoms or of the ancient Roman administration. The church assumed responsibility for dictating the opinions and ordering the conduct of men in every station of life. In the course of time the bishop of Rome, Christ's vice-regent on earth, claimed dominion over both church and state. He strove to make his word final in the moral, intellectual and political spheres. This seemed quite proper since he was the princely head of the earthly Kingdom of God.

The church, founded and officered by the decrees of God, was believed to be the only institution capable of saving the human race from present distress and future punishment. Without its ministrations men on earth were the legitimate prey of the Evil One, and after death their souls would spend eternity in torment. The Catholic sacerdotal system provided the only way of escape. Through the sacraments, divine grace, forgiveness and benefactions were infallibly mediated. From the cradle to the grave, and even to the intermediate purgatorial state beyond, the fostering care of

the church followed all those who made it their spiritual
mother and bowed to its discipline. There was no other
channel by which divine help could flow down to needy
mortals. The church also asserted lordship over men's
minds. As sole mediator of revelation, it was in possession
of all truth. Its Scriptures, its apostolic traditions, the decisions of its councils, and the writings of its orthodox
Fathers were the repositories of divine wisdom. Properly
accredited interpreters had access to these treasures which
they gladly distributed to all seekers ready to receive the
truth in humility and obedience. But heretics and schismatics were anathema; by cherishing error and propagating
dissension they made themselves enemies of God. Intellectual efforts were indeed commendable if directed toward
proper ends. No limits were placed upon the exercise of
human reason if it remained true to the divine mind as disclosed through the church. One's mental energy could never
be turned to better account than when it was employed to
defend the validity or interpret the content of traditional
beliefs.

Thus the hierarchy, the sacramental rites, the ascetic discipline and the dogma of the church continued for centuries
to hold a foremost place in the attention of Christians. Each
of these items represented a very definite heritage from the
past. While no one of them remained absolutely static, they
nevertheless underwent no radical change in character.
Slight alterations in form or function were made from time
to time as new conditions arose, but in the main these devel-

opments served only to entrench more solidly inherited attitudes and opinions. Christian thinkers were generally content to pursue old trails laboriously marked out by their revered predecessors.

I

The medieval mind was much concerned with the doctrine of the hierarchy. This was a perfectly normal consequence of Augustine's theory that the church is the specific means chosen by God to establish his imperial dominion on earth. The effective administration of a world-embracing institution demanded a hierarchy, and a hierarchical system required for its efficient operation a supreme executive in the person of an emperor or a pope. But in the fifth century Western emperors had become too feeble to be either troublesome masters or capable servants of the ecclesiastical establishment. Nor had the disruption of the civil state yet progressed sufficiently far to impress upon Christians the ultimate necessity of providing their own imperial ruler. Thus Augustine was spared the trouble of working out in practice the full implications of his thesis. But the task could not be evaded by his successors, nor could they fail to perceive the direction in which doctrine would have to move if Augustine's vision of the Kingdom of God on earth was to be realized. By gradual stages Christian thinking advanced from Cyprian's and Augustine's notions of an episcopally administered apostolic *imperium* to emphasis upon the supremacy of a single successor of Peter presiding over all ecclesiastical affairs, and ultimately to the explicit affirmation of the lordship of the Roman pontiff over all bishops and princes.

The evolution of papal imperialism from the fifth to the twelfth century is entangled in a network of social, political and ecclesiastical developments that we shall not at present attempt to unravel. It will suffice for our purpose to note certain conditioning factors in the general situation.

At the outset the papal elections rested upon very shaky foundations. The appointment of a successor to a deceased pope, like the choice of bishops for other sees, was in the hands of the local clergy and neighboring bishops, while the Christian populace were privileged to express their approbation or disapproval, a right which they not infrequently exercised in a riotous manner sometimes resulting in bloodshed. When unanimity could not be attained, rival popes contended for the privilege of perpetuating the authority of Peter. The intervention of political rulers was then needed to restore and preserve order. Constantinople was the source to which the church preferred to look for this help, yet more immediate assistance often came from princes of the Goths, Lombards or Franks. Finally, in the eighth century, the supervision of Eastern emperors, who had on occasion grossly abused their prerogative, was deliberately repudiated in favor of Frankish protection.

During these chaotic times the idea of papal jurisdiction over bishops in territories beyond Rome was often very loosely held, if not entirely ignored. In the barbarian kingdoms, even after their rulers had abandoned Arianism for

Catholicism, the local bishops recognized no ecclesiastical head superior to their own Christian princes. As feudalism spread over western Europe the notion of a unified Christendom became still more difficult to maintain. The feudal noble, being a law unto himself, preferred to appoint his own parish priest for the private chapels of the baronial estates. Frequently bishops also were feudal lords who felt scant respect for papal supervision. The structure of society was atomistic, life was nourished chiefly from the soil, the predatory war-lords were both the plunderers and the protectors of property, and the City of God on earth as envisaged by Augustine seemed destined to retire behind the moat of the feudal castle or withdraw into the seclusion of the monastery. Neither the authority of a universal episcopate nor the mandate of a bishop of bishops fitted comfortably into this setting.

Ultimately these divisive energies overreached themselves. Gradually new demands for a larger measure of social solidarity and unification won a hearing. When the aggression of the Saracens and the raids of the Norsemen ceased to be a menace, the feudal nobles, preying upon one another, became a nuisance rather than a protection to life and property. The Crusades provided a channel for a draining off of this belligerent energy from the lands of Europe into the Eastern world. Artisans and traders multiplied with the growth of towns. The importance of the third estate — the bourgeoisie — steadily increased. Money displaced land as a measure of values better suited to the needs of expanding trade and commerce. Rising monarchies slowly subjected the autocratic feudal nobility. The payment of taxes as a form of discharging obligations replaced the former duty of military service pledged by the vassal to his lord. Cultural interests also revived, stimulated by contact with the learning of the Mohammedans, by the widening outlook and increased prosperity resulting from commercial contacts with the East, and by the greater freedom of intercourse now possible for students from different parts of Europe. Universities sprang up, notably at Bologna, Paris and Oxford, whither young men came in their common quest for learning.

Surprising as it may seem, the doctrine of an infallible and unitary Christendom survived, notwithstanding the many heterogeneous and disruptive forces that played all over the surface of medieval civilization, sometimes stirring it to its very depths. Amid all the confusion of the times the church remained the most stable and enduring institution. Supernaturalism continued to be the dominant mode of thought for people in all stations of life. In the last resort safety and truth came from above; they were blessings that man could not hope to procure except through the generosity of the Deity. And the greater the confusion and uncertainty in life, the more one craved a divine anchorage for the soul. Since the church was thought to be the only instrument for mediating God's assistance, its ministrations were indispensable. Its essential unity resided in the people's common faith in the supernatural rather than in any superimposed theory of a centralized ecclesiastical organization. We read back our modern sophistication into that age when we simply accuse the medieval hierarchy of exploiting the laity. It would be nearer the truth to affirm that the lay mind would of necessity have created the hierarchy if Christian tradition had not already provided the people with this indispensable instrument for bringing the help of God into the arena of common life.

Yet the doctrine of hierarchical imperialism was not an original product of the medieval mind, however well it served the demands of that day. Local priests and bishops, rather than a supreme pontiff, were quite sufficient for ordinary needs. Without the momentum of older custom and inherited tradition the imperial way of thinking might never have entered into the medieval picture. This seed grew and bore fruit because nourished by those princes and bishops whose piety fed upon reverence for the glories of the past — the glories of Roman political imperialism and the transcendent majesty of the ideal Kingdom of God. At the outset belief in the supremacy of the papacy was indigenous only to the soil of Italy. From time to time strong popes, with many a long interim when relatively insignificant individuals held office, fostered the doctrine of dominance, at first applying it only to ecclesiastical affairs but ultimately pushing it to its logical conclusion to embrace both church and state. This process began in the fifth century when first Leo and later Gelasius occupied the papal chair and struggled to preserve order amid the confusion that threatened Italy.

Leo was humbled by the thought of assuming the responsibilities of an office which made him head of the universal church to represent " Peter in Peter's see " and wield the authority that Christ himself had conferred upon the Roman bishop. With devout conviction and persistent effort he magnified his high calling for more than twenty years (440–461). Whether it was Attila the Hun, Gaiseric the Vandal, an ecumenical council convened by the order of an Eastern emperor, or a heretical sect in any part of the Christian world that challenged his attention, he rose to the occasion in full confidence that through him Peter spoke the will of Christ. Henceforth, the doctrine of the Roman bishop's supremacy, at least in all matters affecting religion, was a clearly defined and generally known dogma. In the West, if not in the East, its theoretical prestige had been thoroughly established and explicitly affirmed by the imperial edict of Valentinian III in the year 449.

A generation later under Pope Gelasius (492–496) the doctrine was significantly reasserted. He boldly affirmed his superiority over princes, even over the surviving imperial house at Constantinople. This claim was based on the widely recognized principle of the superiority of spiritual to temporal powers, and may well have been inspired by Augustine's doctrine regarding the City of God. Certainly the words of Gelasius have an Augustinian ring: " There are two, O august emperor, by whom principally this world is ruled: the sacred authority of the pontiffs and the royal power. Of these powers that of the priests is so much the more weighty according as they have to render an account even for kings of men in the day of divine judgment. . . . And if it is seemly that the hearts of the faithful should yield submission to all priests generally, who correctly administer divine things, how much the more is obedience due the protector of that see which the highest divinity wished to be pre-eminent over all priests and which consequently the devotion of the universal church perpetually honors." Gelasius did not explicitly affirm the authority of the pope over politics, yet this was certainly implied in a type of thinking that drew no sharp distinction between the natural and the supernatural. The latter really included the former, as it did for Augustine and Christian theologians generally throughout the Middle Ages.

The duty of the political ruler to serve the church was a belief inherited from Ambrose and Augustine. This service was to be rendered at the command of the church and in conformity with its cherished interests. During the succeeding centuries Western Christendom retained this doctrine, but in Italy the secular rulers proved to be a frail staff on which to lean until Charlemagne appeared upon the scene toward the close of the eighth century. Two hundred years earlier Gregory the Great (590–604) had so insistently besought the Eastern Emperor to come to the aid of the Roman church that Gregory virtually exalted the power of the state above that of the church, thus laying the foundation for the doctrine of the divine right of kings. They, like Saul of old, were God's anointed. To criticize them even for their faults was to sin against God and invite the divine judgment of him who had established the kingship (*Pastoral Rule*, III, 4). Gregory was similarly deferential towards praetors and exarchs. Since their civil authority was God-given, the bishop ventured to remind them that by forcibly suppressing heretics or rendering other aid to the church they could acquire an " increase of glory with the Creator " (*Epistles*, I, 74).

It was in practice rather than theory that Gregory made his most significant contribution to the doctrine of papal supremacy. He accepted without question the Augustinian view of the church as a divine and infallible institution, the only teacher of revealed truth beyond whose pale salvation was impossible, and the authentic though preliminary manifestation of the Kingdom of God on earth. To this faith he added Leo's consciousness of the grave responsibilities of the bishop of Rome. As successor to Peter, Gregory felt himself to be the shepherd of all souls and " servant of the servants of God." With rare consistency and devotion, reinforced by monastic piety, Gregory applied himself to the practical task of making the moral and spiritual influence of the church prevail throughout the Western world for the good of both common men and those of high estate. That he failed to stress more forcibly worldly power and official position is not surprising when we recall the fact that for Gregory society seemed so overwhelmed by mounting disasters — the devastation of Italy by the Lombards, the recurrences of deadly pestilence and the general disruption of life — that the day of final judgment was believed to be imminent. To establish control over an earthly prince, whose dominion was soon to end by the act of God, would have been a waste of energy. But to make the church a more seaworthy ship for the transport of immortal souls to heaven did in reality insure its supremacy in the thinking of the Middle Ages. For his service in this respect Gregory has not improperly been called the creator of medieval Catholicism.

Gregory's expectation of an early end of the world remained unrealized. The church continued to be buffeted by the billows throughout two more stormy centuries before the doctrine of papal supremacy made any real headway. In the meantime there had been a subtle shift of emphasis in both religious and political thinking. In the fifth century Gelasius had envisaged the government of the world in terms of two administrative powers, the church and the emperor. In the ninth century the imagery had significantly changed. Now men thought more commonly of two authorities by which God governed the church: the ecclesiastical hierarchy and the prince. In this shift there was both a loss and a gain for the papacy, but in the end the advantages far outweighed the disadvantages. Henceforth church and state appeared to be an essential entity rather than rival institutions. Religious obligations were imposed upon princes as an integral part of their regal duties. When kings were thus necessarily church-men, the pope had only to assert his supremacy within the church in order to justify his right to control secular rulers. But at the outset harmony was more important than conflict for both ecclesiastics and politicians.

The harmonious relations between Charlemagne and the papacy strikingly illustrate this new trend in doctrine. Prince and bishop labored together to restore to western Europe an empire that would perpetuate the civil authority of ancient Rome and at the same time establish, though in a somewhat denatured form, the Kingdom of God portrayed by Augustine. Quite naturally Augustine's *City of God* was Charlemagne's favorite book. Church and state shared a common responsibility for maintaining a Christian civilization. Kings or emperors had a care for the appointment and conduct of the clergy and for enforcing the divine law inculcated by the church; while clerics, and especially popes, confirmed the titles of princes, or even played a part in their selection, and anointed them to rule " by the grace of God." Secularism, as such, had no conspicuous place in the picture. Perhaps it would be more accurate to say that secular activities were so generously baptized by ecclesiastical sanctions that it became impossible to draw a sharp distinction between the two interests. Kings ruled by divine right but under the aegis of the church, while the church was protected by the royal authority which it had helped to create.

Beneath the surface of these events there was an underlying motivation of which men in that day were perhaps hardly conscious, and the full significance of which even later interpreters have not always duly recognized. A subtle influence emanated from the widespread sense of the importance of law in the construction and maintenance of civilization. This feeling might be less a doctrine than a sentiment, and its expression might lack explicit formulation; nevertheless it exalted the sanctity of custom, in loyalty to which the individual and society found the surest guaranties of safety.

During the period of anarchy that prevailed in Italy throughout the eighth century, popes had been compelled to assume chief responsibility for all affairs pertaining to the welfare of the people. While the procedure rested on no formal statutes of either state or church, the wider activities of popes had become an established custom in response to the needs of the times. In fact, legally, Italy was still a possession of the Eastern emperor, of whom the bishop of Rome was a subject. Thus current practice and formal law were at variance with each other. An impasse was avoided by a drastic but inevitable action. Custom raised itself to the dignity of law in the fabrication of the famous document known as the Donation of Constantine. The first Christian Emperor was credited with having so far anticipated the outcome of subsequent history that nearly five hundred years earlier he had handed over to the bishop of Rome full sovereignty in the West by declaring it quite improper that " an earthly emperor should have jurisdiction over a celestial emperor of the Christian religion." This was merely an ideal statement of what had been transformed by custom into actual fact. The new doctrine was not superimposed upon the world by the arbitrary will of the papacy; it was essentially the formulation of what had come to be established practice. Historically adjudged, the document was certainly a forgery, but as a product of its own day it rang true to the contemporary life-situation.

The so-called pseudo-Isidorian Decretals had a similar genesis. They were a product of the needs of the Frankish church in the period of confusion following the death of Charlemagne. Custom had now established beyond question popular respect for Rome as the original source of Catholic truth and the ancient home of law and order. The Roman church was universally revered as the mother of Western Christendom, however independently Frankish bishops and princes might act in their several jurisdictions. When Frankish Christianity became conscious of its shortcomings and restive under multiplying forms of exploitation by its worldly minded clerics and princes, the more religiously sensitive minds looked to Rome as the normal court of appeal for the restoration of a more spiritual order. The Decretals in question were a product of this popular urge. They embodied as law emanating from Rome the efforts already current to exalt religious above secular interests and to curb the authority of feudally minded metropolitans. At the same time the authority of the papacy was augmented by first having ascribed to it appellative, and later legislative, jurisdiction. But that result was incidental to the more primary purpose of legalizing reforms that the Franks themselves had learned to desire.

The Cluniac reform in the tenth century directed Christian thinking along the same highway to Rome. The attempt to revive spiritual life in the monasteries spread in time to the church at large. Powerful and well-meaning Saxon emperors in the tenth and eleventh centuries did much to restore decency in the church, but at the same time brought it more completely under bondage to secular powers. Their successors were only too ready to abuse this authority. Then reformers perceived that the older ideals of spiritual excellence in Christianity were being thwarted anew by secular interests. Again the remedy was sought in a return to Rome, the ancient source of religious authority. This involved a further exaltation of papal supremacy. Thus only can one understand the forces that precipitated the long struggle for power between popes and emperors, a conflict familiar to every student of medieval history.

In the heat generated by this controversy the spiritual ideal may often have been obscured, while the desire to establish the imperial authority of the pope may seem to have been the dominant concern. But beneath the surface there was always the powerful urge to make the church the infallible guardian of truth and the sole ark of salvation for mankind. The ancient paths of thought seemed to be the only safe road to travel. The church fought for the supremacy of spiritual over secular authority, never for a moment conceiving the possibility that the two could exist and function separately in the same world.

Papal ascendancy had by the opening of the fourteenth century reached its zenith under Boniface VIII (1294–1303). Its cornerstone was the inherited doctrine of Roman imperialism embracing both church and state. In his famous bull, *Unam sanctam,* Boniface tersely reaffirmed the old principle that had been gathering momentum since the days of Augustine and of Charlemagne: " Both the material and the spiritual swords are in the power of the church, but the latter is wielded for the church and the former by the church; the one by priests, the other by kings and soldiers, but at the command or with the approval of the priest." In establishing this doctrine popes triumphed over emperors, but only to find themselves confronted by a new secular power in the person of the kings of the rising nations of Europe.

Even so, nationalism did not at first perceive the propriety of making religion and politics distinct interests. Still a long way off was the day of formal separation between church and state. The decline of papal prestige in the fourteenth century was not due to any essential change in doctrine. The traditional way of thinking remained intact. The kings of the new nations simply took over the responsibility for directing the affairs of the church as an essential part of the duties of kingship. The royal power thus supplanted the ecclesiastical hierarchy in the administration of both political and religious affairs. Liberation of spiritual interests from political domination still awaited the dawn of a new age in the history of Christian doctrine.

II

During the Middle Ages the chief purpose of Christian doctrine was to justify the believer's hope of attaining unto heavenly bliss, and to define the means by which this hope could be surely realized. Without a properly constituted and carefully regulated hierarchical system to guard and operate sacred rites, religion could not fulfill its divine mission. Sacerdotalism was fundamental to the success of the whole Christian enterprise. And the necessary concomitant of priestly activity was sacramentalism. Hence the doctrine of the sacraments occupied a large place beside the doctrine of the hierarchy. In this respect also thinking moved along old ways to which earlier generations of Christians had become thoroughly habituated.

The sanctity of the sacraments, especially the initiatory rite of baptism and the repeated observance of the eucharist, had become firmly established within the mind of Christendom during the second century. Reverence for these sacred rites had been further enhanced by the prominence given them in the thinking of ecclesiastical leaders like Cyprian, Ambrose and Augustine. Not only the ordinary worshiper but even the most intellectually inclined theologian, if he were orthodox, accepted both baptism and the eucharist as divinely authorized acts indispensable to the existence of the church. If one did not so think, membership in the true church was an impossibility. The practices were valid in their own right quite apart from the interpretation placed upon the rites by the theologians. The latter merely perpetuated and expounded what God himself had instituted. Sacramental doctrine was secondary to — one might say in some instances merely a by-product of — the operations of the cultus.

Once the validity of the ceremonies was admitted, the meaning attaching to them might vary widely according to circumstances and individuals. Eastern thought tended to dwell upon the notion of mystery as a means by which some sort of union was effected between the Deity and the devotee. In the West, on the other hand, where the idea of communion was less general, preference was given to the more juridical conception of obligation to be discharged and favor to be bestowed. Since the rites had been inherited from the East, it continued to be proper to speak of a mystery (*mysterium*) as an esoteric act whose meaning might transcend human comprehension, but the notion of sacrament (*sacramentum*) or sacrifice (*sacrificium*) was more congenial to the Western mind. The underlying idea was much the same whether one spoke of a " sacrament," by which God conferred something on man, or a " sacrifice," by which something was offered to God on man's behalf. The sacred rite symbolized, pledged, confirmed or actually insured the validity of a contract by which God removed guilt, conferred grace or bestowed his favor in return for a gift.

Systematic phrasing of sacramental doctrine was relatively late in making its appearance. Since the fundamental principle had been universally established at an early date, for a long time sacramental practices grew in number and esteem unhindered by any body of formally defined opinions on the subject. Even Augustine failed to unify this aspect of his thinking, which in fact was marred by some notable inconsistencies. Every time God had expressed his purposes in revelation, the symbols or signs thus pertaining to divine things were, Augustine said, properly called " sacraments " (*Epistle* 138. 7). When he was speaking generally, apparently he could apply the same term to every act of the Christian cultus and could regard each as indispensable in its place. But baptism and the eucharist seem to have been the only rites absolutely required by everybody for salvation. The remaining sacraments were more in the nature of privileges or were suited to certain exigencies, such as priestly ordination, exorcism, penance, marriage.

The strain of Neoplatonic absolutism in Augustine, which he developed so extremely in his doctrines of prevenient grace and double predestination — predestination to life and predestination to death — if logically applied to his interpretation of the sacraments would seem to have made them quite incidental, if not entirely unnecessary. But a bishop, responsible for initiating people into the church and providing means for nourishing ecclesiastical piety, could not dispense with traditional rites. Therefore he stoutly affirmed that baptismal regeneration, even the baptism of infants, was necessary for salvation, and that participation in the eucharist actually bestowed a divine grace otherwise unattainable. In practice it had to be assumed that man had free will to choose whether or not he would submit to the saving ordinances of the church. And, if he did submit, his act could hardly fail to be accounted meritorious in God's sight even though this inference was out of accord with the philosophical premises of Augustine's thinking. In the actual conduct of the church, ritual procedures had to be given the right of way.

Augustine's rigid insistence on the necessity of the sacramental mechanism may seem to us strangely inconsistent with his deep spirituality and his personal experience of communion with God. But evidently he felt no serious difficulty at this point, nor did it furnish any insurmountable obstacle to his readers in the Middle Ages. They readily ignored his spiritual moods, while leaning heavily on him to support their notion of the thoroughly sacramental character of the Christian program of redemption. They yearned for a religion of objective reality mediated through sensible channels. Especially was this true with reference to the elements in the eucharist. In this again Augustine's language was confusing, or was at least capable of different interpretations. While he dwelt upon the spiritual significance of Christ's words in instituting the rite, and spoke of sacraments as " visible signs of divine things," he did admit that " after a fashion the sacrament of Christ's body is Christ's body." It was true in a certain sense that when Christ said " This is my body " he actually " carried his body " to the communicants at the Last Supper. His presence in the eucharist was certainly objective, and Augustine's frequent repetition of traditional language, implying somehow a miraculous change in the bread and the wine, made it easy for his successors, like Gregory the Great, to hold to a thoroughly divine presence in the elements.

The sacrificial interpretation of the eucharist received a strong stimulus from Gregory, whose popularity in medieval times was second only to that of Augustine. Indeed, Gregory's interpretation of Augustine did much to insure the latter's wide influence even when, as in the case of the sacraments, he did not specifically ground his teaching on the authority of the African Father. Yet he perpetuated in part the spiritual strain in Augustine, while dwelling more fondly upon realism and resorting freely to allegorical language. Christ was actually present in the eucharistic sacrament in which the communicant partook of the flesh and blood of the Lamb with both the mouth of the body and the mouth of the heart.

But it was in his sacrificial view of the rite that Gregory made his chief contribution to later thinking. The body and blood of Christ were daily offered to God in the mystery of the sacred oblation. It was Christ's " flesh that is divided for the salvation of the people, his blood that is poured, not now into the hands of unbelievers but into the mouths of the faithful. Hence let us think what this sacrifice means for us which ever imitates for our absolution the passion of the only begotten Son " (*Dial.* IV, 58). Its efficacy for both the living and the dead was immeasurable. When the priest uttered the formula of institution the very heavens were opened, the angelic choirs responded, earth and heaven were joined and things visible and invisible became one.

With the heritages from Augustine and Gregory in hand, later medieval thinkers could have no serious doubts about the course to be pursued in their further development of sacramental doctrine. They had only to teach people generally the correct forms to be used, to clarify opinion regarding the exact number to be observed, and to indicate more particularly the significance of the rites as a means of preparing souls for heaven. In the main the task was practical rather than speculative, and was often more significant for ethics than for doctrine in the stricter sense of that term. But in medieval times ethical theory and theological dogma were as inseparably interwoven as were the doctrines of church and state.

Proper procedure in the observance of a sacrament involved the services of an authorized agent — a priest or bishop. God acted only through the official ministry of his church. No clergyman, no sacrament. This attitude was quite different from that of earlier times when the virtue of a sacrament had resided in the act itself without reference to a clerical ministrant. But those were the days before the doctrine of the hierarchy had been perfected. Baptism was the only rite to which any measure of the older freedom adhered; it might still be performed by a layman, even by a woman, but only in case of a grave emergency. Not the individual clergyman but his official status validated the sacramental act. Personally he might be ignorant, wrong in his opinions, or even immoral in his conduct, but if he were in regular standing and used the prescribed formulas, the sacrament was effective. It derived its virtue from the divine institution by which it was sponsored, however frail the human agent might be.

The sacraments remained indefinite in number until the twelfth century, but varying opinions apparently caused no great anxiety. Baptism and the eucharist had been recognized from the first, and later a great variety of religious practices and ceremonies was freely termed sacraments, though of distinctly lesser dignity. This was still the custom with Augustine and with Gregory. But a growing concern for ecclesiastical regularity prompted an effort to fix upon an exact number. In the eleventh century five were specified by influential thinkers — baptism, confirmation, the eucharist, (extreme) unction and marriage. Presently two more were added — clerical orders and penance. Henceforth the sacred number seven prevailed, although it was not given formal sanction until the fifteenth century.

Each sacrament served a distinct purpose that gave it meaning for the Christian life and supplied the basis for a doctrinal interpretation. But there was one underlying principle common to all thinking about the sacraments as a whole. In line with the prevailing religious temper of the period, God was assumed to be the unconditioned operating power active in all these rites. Their significance derived from the divine act in and of itself, *ex opere operato*. It conferred or conveyed grace solely by virtue of the omnipotence of the Deity. What was required of the recipient? Augustinian absolutism had answered that nothing was required, but if faith were lacking in the devotee he would be harmed rather than benefited by the sacrament. Medieval thinking relaxed this rigidity in two directions. It was conceded that a willingness to receive grace made one eligible for its benefits, and the proper attitude of the recipient was accounted meritorious. The worshiper himself did that which deserved a reward, and hence received an additional grace by virtue of his own act, *ex opere operantis*. Divine reward and human merit thus went hand in hand.

The distinctive functions of the several sacraments are too well known to call for detailed exposition. Baptism effected regeneration, wiped out all previous sins whether personal or inherited, and removed the burden of guilt. Confirmation, especially after infant baptism had become the common practice, gave fresh strength to the soul in its further conflict with evil. Extreme unction expiated any remaining sins and paved the way for a safe entrance into the realms beyond. Ordination secured to the church a valid clergy. The sacrament of matrimony, making the family a divine institution and establishing a relationship as indissoluble as the union between Christ and the church, was meant also for the good of the ecclesiastical institution. It brought all future generations within the jurisdiction of the church and thus secured to it a continuing membership. All of these rites, performed but once in the lifetime of the individuals involved, belonged to a somewhat different category of values from those attaching to the eucharist and penance, sacraments that were repeated again and again in the experience of the faithful.

Of all the sacred rites in the medieval church, the eucharist was by far the most important both to the ordinary man and to the ecclesiastical dignitaries. The whole Catholic system of thinking and morals centered about this celebration. It was the great source of inspiration for piety and it involved theologians in some of their most intricate speculations. The conceptions of sacrament and sacrifice were both strongly emphasized; the eucharist bestowed God's grace upon needy men and was also a propitiation for their sins. Even those who did not personally receive the rite derived benefit therefrom as a sacrifice offered for their salvation whether they were present or absent, living or dead. When the elements were consecrated the worshiper experienced the elation felt in the presence of the majestic miracle by which the ordinary elements of bread and wine were transformed into the actual body and blood of Christ. Thus Christ became as realistic a presence for the community of medieval believers as he had been for his personal companions during his earthly career in Palestine.

Belief in the transformation of the elements was a commonly accepted doctrine. But the nature of the change invited speculation. Augustine had inclined toward a spiritual and symbolical interpretation of its meaning, but Gregory had less hesitation in accepting a more realistic and physical conception. Thinkers during the Middle Ages struggled with the problem. Some of them, Berengar for example, coming out boldly against the irrationality involved in accepting the notion of a literal change, insisted that Christ was spiritually rather than corporeally present. But the trend of opinion being overwhelmingly against Berengar's skepticism, he was forced to recant on pain of condemnation for heresy. Henceforth the doctrine of literal transubstantiation held undisputed sway in all orthodox circles and was made an official dogma of the church at the fourth Lateran Council in 1215. Discussion thereafter confined itself to incidental questions. Could there be a change in substance but not in form? Was the whole Christ in every particle of the two elements, thus making it unnecessary for the laity to be given the cup? How could one appraise the magnitude of the divine mystery involved in the transcendent miracle?

In the sphere of morality penance was especially important for medieval thinking. This sacrament provided a means of keeping life up to date in the matter of man's personal effort to stand right with God. The value of virtuous conduct, tested by ascetic practices, had been recognized at an early date within Christianity. Although Augustine stressed good works and inculcated self-discipline, his theological position compelled him to reject the idea of man's ability to acquire virtue on his own account. Hence he made all merit a divine donation: " God crowns our merits by crowning his own gifts." Gregory restored the balance between human effort and divine reward. He tacitly rejected the Augustinian doctrine of man's utter helplessness over against God's almightiness, and rephrased the relationship in terms of characteristic Roman judicial thinking. God was still almighty, not because he was the Neoplatonic absolute of philosophy, but because he was the righteous ruler of the universe to whom obedience was due. He was the inexorable judge who exacted a suitable penalty for every trespass against his majesty.

Gregory's doctrine of penance was built upon the assumption that no sin can escape punishment. God, writes Gregory, " never leaves a fault without taking vengeance on it; for either man himself by penance punishes it in himself, or God assisting man in punishment smites it " (*Moralia,* IX, 54). Thus penance became a " second baptism " effective for washing away guilt, a means by which man paid the penalty due his sin, and a technique for securing release from postbaptismal transgressions. One had, as it were, to pave one's own way to heaven by penitential discipline. In this emphasis Gregory was undoubtedly largely influenced by his monastic training as well as by his heritage from Roman legalism. Thus the penitential system, revived and further developed by Gregory, became a conspicuous medieval doctrine.

In the original form of the practice God required that the penitent should clearly prove his sincerity. He had to have a contrite heart, to make a candid confession, and to render an appropriate satisfaction for his sins. At least once a year confession was to be made to a priest who pronounced the proper formula of absolution conveying the divine grace and releasing the confessor from eternal punishment, but only on condition that adequate satisfaction be rendered to God either in this life or in purgatory. In the case of those still living the demand for satisfaction was met by humbling one's self in prayer, by punishing the flesh through fasting, by parting with one's possessions for the help of the needy, or by other worthy acts such as making pilgrimages to holy places or building monuments, particularly churches.

Rendering satisfaction was a conception that conformed readily to the customs and thinking of feudal times, and its natural counterpart was the practice of granting indulgences. The task of paying in full one's own debts, in an age which magnified the debtor's obligations but often removed his actual ability to pay quite beyond his reach, demanded remedial measures. Under these circumstances the duty had to be passed on to others who possessed the necessary resources. The church, endowed as it was by a superabundance of merit built up from the excellencies of Christ and the saints, generously provided from this reserve help for all needy persons. Those sinners who were unable or indisposed to discharge the often burdensome obligations involved in their personal indebtedness were offered an opportunity to draw upon the treasury of merit at the disposal of the church. This phase of penitential doctrine encouraged the practice of granting indulgences dispensed by the pope and his authorized representatives — a custom that in course of time proved morally degenerating to the individual and threatened to wreck even the power of the papacy.

III

While the hierarchy and the sacraments loomed large in medieval Christendom, the more speculative aspects of doctrine were not entirely neglected. Even in the most intellectually barren periods of medieval history the quest of the individual for larger knowledge was never totally absent. But it was the pursuit of the few rather than of the many, and for a long time was little known outside of the cathedral and monastic schools. Since educational work was carried on exclusively in Latin, its results were not available for the rank and file who conversed only in the vernaculars. Education of the masses was rarely or never encouraged by either the ecclesiastical or the political authorities. This circumstance was advantageous to the scholars, in that it left them free to pursue theological problems without incurring the danger of a popular furor, yet it limited their audiences and often left their best efforts without a fertile soil in which to germinate and bear normal fruit.

The general use of Latin had, however, one very beneficial result. Since it made such knowledge as was available a common possession of all scholars, learning could pass freely across all national boundaries. Teachers and students readily moved about from one educational center to another, thus giving to medieval civilization one of its most substantial bonds of unity. The future history of Europe might have taken a very different course if in the early days it had been possible to extend education beyond clerical circles to include all classes. There might then have developed a common language for the literary expression of new cultural attainments. The influence of a common speech in cementing the diverse racial elements and widely scattered territories in America is as fortunate as it is noteworthy. Perhaps a similar unification of Europe could have been effected if education at the outset had been able to forsake the cloister and permeate the life of the populace. But even if the pursuit of learning was not general in the early medieval period, its limited survival was nevertheless very important for the history of the church.

The educational practice and policy of the medieval church, like its hierarchical and sacramental developments, remained closely bound to the traditions of the past. The intellectual leaders showed very little inclination or ability to mark out new highways for the exercise of their mental powers. Aggressive thinking on the debatable problems of dogma that earlier had agitated the philosophical minds of the Eastern church, and had found a worthy Western representative in Augustine, now became relatively quiescent. It is true that dialectic, along with grammar and rhetoric — the famous *trivium* inherited from the Roman system of education — continued to be taught. Thus a foundation was ostensibly laid for the exercise of the rational faculty, since skill in dialectic was assumed to be a preparation for philosophical speculation. But the allurements of education were not sufficiently enticing to deliver reason from the fetters binding it to the rock of authority. While there were various incentives prompting the more alert minds to activity, there were many counter forces that imposed limitations

upon freedom of thinking and dulled the edge of man's intellect.

The intellectual darkness pervading the earlier centuries of the Middle Ages has often been exaggerated. A reaction from this derogatory appraisal has long been overdue, and it need not surprise us to find that new appraisers sometimes tend to overestimate the virtues of their rehabilitated heroes. The attempts being made in certain quarters today to reconstruct Christian doctrine on a dichotomy of reason and revelation unified by means of dialectic certainly has a genuinely medieval flavor. But whether this procedure heightens respect for the intellectualism of medieval thinkers, or is a reflection upon the quality of twentieth-century intelligence, remains an open question. It is conceivable that difficulties and frustrations in modern life may simply have stampeded thinking, driving it to seek refuge in the fortifications of a new " Dark Ages," rather than spurring it on to the conquest of stronger citadels for the mind.

All medieval thinkers traveled the authoritarian highway to truth. This did not mean that they always rode in the same vehicle, or found the going uniformly comfortable, or progressed at the same rate of speed. But they all had in view the same goal — the acquisition of truth authenticated ultimately by God himself. Since deity was the fountainhead of all knowledge, the church was the divinely established institution for mediating heavenly wisdom to man. Individual reason might come into some conflict with the authority of one or another ecclesiastical agency, or the relative priority of reason and tradition might be debated, but the ultimate harmony between true knowledge and true faith was rarely or never questioned. It could not be otherwise in an age when supernaturalism dominated all minds. We shall find ourselves quite incapacitated to understand the development of theological doctrines in the Middle Ages if we read back into that day anything of the modern state of mind that makes possible the conception of an essential contrast between scientific knowledge and religious beliefs. Where supernatural thinking prevailed, it was as impossible to separate knowledge from faith as it was to separate church from state, or piety from sacraments. All things were bound together in one transcendental mind whose authority governed every true thought and every proper deed of mankind.

On the other hand, the function of individual human intelligence, the content of particular traditional beliefs, and the validity of specific ecclesiastical authorities might well be questioned under any given set of circumstances. These problems furnished medieval theologians their task and circumscribed their thinking. Some typical illustrations of their work will be sufficient to indicate the general direction in which they moved and the distinctive forces that controlled their activities.

Gregory the Great had passed on to the seventh century a somewhat de-intellectualized Augustine. The latter had not only made large use of reason in his formulation of dogma, but had also advocated discipline in the " liberal arts " of Roman educational tradition as a preparation for theological study. Yet for Augustine, the Neoplatonist, reason was more in the nature of an immediate intellectual perception than a conviction resting on a process of logic, and as a bishop he felt more and more inclined to insist on the primacy of faith based on the authority of ecclesiastical teaching. In any event, reason was a gift from God, not a creation of the human mind, and therefore it followed that " we believe in order that we may know, we do not know in order that we may believe."

With Gregory reason practically disappeared from the picture. To believe that which seemed reasonable was not meritorious; if Christianity had not offered men truth that transcended reason it would have been unworthy of admiration. Gregory correspondingly discounted educational ideals, even to the extent of advising against the teaching of grammar. He would set in the foreground implicit acceptance of Scripture and the creed, supplemented by the decrees of the four general councils. As time passed, the specific norms of authority were gradually multiplied by Gregory's successors until they included the opinions of the approved Fathers, especially the four great Western " doctors," Ambrose, Jerome, Augustine and Gregory, the decisions of local councils, the judgments of prominent bishops, the codification of church law, and finally the *ex cathedra* pronouncements of the papacy. This line of thinking reached specific formulation with Hincmar, Bishop of Reims, in the latter part of the ninth century.

In the meantime a parallel development had been in progress. It perpetuated the educational tradition by means of the wide use of textbooks that had been prepared by Boethius and Cassiodorus, two distinguished Christian scholars of

Italy in the sixth century. The work of the former was especially influential in popularizing the dialectical method of Aristotle among medieval scholars. This remained their chief concern for the next two centuries, thus keeping alive the older rhetorical tradition of the Roman schools. But its emphasis was upon logic rather than oratory. Reason disciplined itself in the use of syllogisms, while it made slight if any effort to discover new truth by means of rational processes of thought. Skill in logic seemed of itself to be the crown of mental discipline.

The speculative aspects of philosophic tradition also survived, especially in remote corners of the monastic world, where remnants of Platonism, Aristotelianism and Neoplatonism were occasionally exhibited and refurbished by the more hardy intellectuals like John the Scot. Platonic idealism, especially as mediated through Augustine, and the popular Neoplatonic treatise that purported to have been composed by Dionysius the Areopagite, gave birth to two types of doctrine. Both sought reality in the realm of transcendentalism, one relying upon rational processes and the other upon the satisfactions of contemplation and emotion for the attainment of ultimate knowledge. The former issued in a way of thinking that is appropriately called " Realism." Reality was believed to reside in universal ideas existing prior to and embracing all concrete things. Thinking moved from universals to particulars, not *vice versa*. In a world of disorder such as that of early medieval times, and in an age when empirical science was unknown, it is not surprising that earnest minds should have tried to pull down order and truth out of the idealized upper regions. Periods of social chaos always tempt men's minds to seek escape to the freer air of transcendentalism. A second alternative was resort to mysticism as the most direct avenue to communion with God, who was the ultimate reality. Many medieval theologians chose the mystical path.

From the ninth to the thirteenth century the stream of intellectual life in western Europe was augmented by several fresh tributaries flowing into it from different sources. The result was a marked increase in both depth and variety of doctrinal interests. Arabian scholars in Spain brought to the West Christian learning from the famous schools at Bagdad and Damascus. A new zeal for intellectual pursuits, gradually spreading north of the Pyrenees, penetrated even to Rome when the Archbishop of Reims became Pope Sylvester II at the end of the tenth century. Influential Christian schools, like those of Reims and Chartres, disseminated the new learning throughout Western Christendom. The process was accelerated by the rise of universities and by the newly established Dominican and Franciscan orders that ultimately developed, along with their preaching propaganda, a lively interest in teaching. It was also a period of awakening interest in moral reform, which stimulated a new sense of individual responsibility for the ordering of conduct and involved the necessity of thinking as well as acting in accordance with personal convictions. Papal interference with the freedom of the schools, that might have proved troublesome, was largely held in abeyance by the fact that the energies of aggressive popes were pretty well exhausted in the more immediate struggle between church and state for supremacy within the expanding medieval civilization. Under these circumstances the schoolmen found a favorable opportunity to make a large place for themselves in the narrower circle of the scholars.

The dialectical heritage from Aristotle, as a tool for expounding or defending theological beliefs, was not necessarily inconsistent with either realism or mysticism, unless the method was pressed to radical extremes or valued chiefly for its own sake. Then it became suspect, especially among the mystics. Sharp criticisms were often urged against the vanity and futility of syllogistic gymnastics. But Aristotelian influence did not confine itself to formal logic as originally derived from Boethius. The new learning had provided a better acquaintance with the content as well as the form of Aristotelian science and philosophy. In one direction the outcome was a swinging away from the widely current mode of thought that assumed the reality of universals only, from which by processes of deductive reasoning one arrived at particular truths. On the other hand, under the inspiration of Aristotle's empiricism, some thinkers affirmed that universals were mere words totally lacking in reality. This was to be found only in concrete things themselves. Representatives of this opinion are called " Nominalists."

When one proceeded inductively from particular substances to universal ideas, and conditioned the truth of the latter by knowledge of the former, one of two results seemed inevitable. Either knowledge derived from observation took precedence over faith based on revelation, or reason and faith had to be treated as independent phenomena not necessarily harmonious with each other. Neither alternative proved generally acceptable to the early scholastic theologians, who could employ with zest the Aristotelian dialectic but were unable to give reason the free reign required by the empirical methods of Aristotle.

By the end of the eleventh century the intellectual urge among the schoolmen had grown too strong to be suppressed, and the pursuit of learning was becoming increasingly popular. The guardians of Christian doctrine had to assume further responsibility for mediating between the new learning and traditional dogma, between knowledge and revelation, between reason and authority. Even though they generally took the " realist " as against the " nominalist " position, they could not maintain intellectual respectability for theology if they totally ignored the content of Aristotelian philosophy with which educated persons were becoming increasingly familiar. This neglect was as impossible for them as it has been for theologians during the last half century to ignore the findings of the modern physical and social sciences. To abandon revelation for reason, or to deny reason any rights whatsoever, were possible extremes. But neither proved generally acceptable among the schoolmen although the latter attitude had its noteworthy representatives, especially among theologians who leaned heavily toward mysticism.

On that great *via media,* where reason is made the servant of authority, where knowledge and faith are skilfully harmonized, and where an earnest attempt is made to show that the enlarging wisdom of the age only increases one's reverence for the reinterpreted teachings of the church, on that highway one meets the well-known scholastic theologians, Anselm, Abelard, Peter Lombard, Albertus Magnus, and the prince of all medieval modernists, Thomas Aquinas, who within fifty years of his death was canonized by the pope. What a different fate was in store for a new generation of Catholic modernists at the opening of the twentieth century! It was their misfortune to appear upon the scene after the system of Catholic dogma had crystallized as rigidly as had the hierarchy and the sacraments, while Thomas and his predecessors lived in an age when the task of providing traditional beliefs with suitable intellectual reinforcements was still in its incipient stages.

The scholastic systematizers of doctrine did not find their pathway strewn with roses. The few daring or incautious spirits who followed reason so consistently that they ventured to revise or reject traditional beliefs, as did Berengar on the Eucharist and Roscelin on the Trinity, quickly incurred condemnation for heresy. Contemporary scholars, bishops, local councils and popes ever stood ready to pronounce the harsh verdict. The very assumption that faith was capable of, or required, rational exposition seemed to some pious people an insult to revealed truth and an offense against the dignity of authority. Also the effort to mingle secular Aristotelian knowledge with the divine wisdom of the church was sharply condemned more than once, even by the papacy. But the genius of Thomas Aquinas, the great scholar of the Dominican Order, proved equal to the Herculean task of effecting an acceptable synthesis of reason and faith that not only satisfied the demands of both revelation and authority, but also allowed breathing space for mysticism.

The "modernist" theologian in any age is essentially a harmonizer, and incisive thinkers will always detect inherent inconsistencies in his synthesis. To them the mixture is artificial, if not indeed an incentive to obscurantism. Even Thomas, the "angelic doctor," did not escape criticism, especially from scholars of the Franciscan Order, who, however, were often modernists in their own way. Bonaventura, the "seraphic doctor" and contemporary of Thomas, objected in particular to the lack of stress on vital religion involved in the Thomist rationalism. Thomas had conceded that logic, while it adequately substantiated the beliefs of the church about God, could not give direct knowledge of him. That was an attainment capable of realization only in the life to come. Now one lived, as it were, by the substance of things hoped for and not by the experience of their realization. As a matter of fact, the mysticism of Thomas was somewhat formal and shallow, and quite unsatisfactory to one who craved a realistic sense of the divine presence, an experience highly prized by many pious souls of that day. Thomas had robbed man's seraphic spirit of its wings and Bonaventura stoutly protested. The latter did not despise sense perception, whose values he learned from Aristotle, but he did insist on giving primacy to Augustine's mystical notion of personal knowledge of God. To deprive the Christian of this divine illumination was to sever the vital nerve of all true piety. Future generations of medieval mystics continued to follow this course even when they did not take up arms against Thomas. Eckhart tersely phrased their fundamental position: "My eye and God's eye are one — one seeing, one knowing, one loving."

Duns Scotus, the "subtle doctor," attacked Thomas from the opposite quarter. It appeared that Thomas had not been sufficiently scientific; he had not always pursued hairsplitting dialectic with proper diligence or to adequate conclusions. Thus scholasticism now began the unconscious process of undermining itself by disclosing the variant opinions that could result from further application of its rational methods. Someone would surely perceive that reason seemed incapable of making good its claim to establish certainty of belief. Fundamentalists always take delight in holding up to ridicule the divergences and disagreements among representatives of modernism. And if modernists are betrayed by their zeal for truth into claiming finality for their conclusions, as though their opinions were a new infallible dogma, they will always be an easy mark for their critics. Infallible dogmas on the one hand, and conclusions arrived at by empirical reasoning on the other, are, strictly speaking, incommensurables. But that fact had not been perceived in the time of Duns Scotus. Divergent conclusions among scholastic theologians could not fail to lessen their influence in an age when finality was still the supreme religious quest.

By the fifteenth century medieval life, and even its religious interests, had become far too complex to remain voluntarily confined within the limits of any unified logical system of doctrine. In the main, thinking still pursued old highways to the authoritative City of God. The propriety of liberating reason to pursue its individualistic course, unfettered by superimposed tradition, seemed unworthy of recognition. The more numerous the divergences of opinion became, the more desirable and necessary did it seem to ecclesiastical leaders that uniformity in dogma, as in the regulation of the hierarchy and the administration of the sacraments, needed to be enforced by the superior authority of the church.

A new group of schoolmen, starting with William of Occam, lent momentum, though quite unconsciously, to the movement for official supervision of dogma. These scholars, by reviving the nominalism of Roscelin and relegating the activities of reason to concretely observable things, gave empiricism a new lease on life. Reason was thereby freed to operate in the natural sphere, provided it did not trespass upon the preserves of faith. The Occamists had no disposition to permit rationalism to wander into forbidden paths. Theological truth, guaranteed by revelation, was of a higher order than rational truth. Thus reason and revelation, philosophy and theology, lived apart and in peace with one another.

The truce was more apparent than real. Even if reason kept the peace by refraining from attack on faith's pronouncements, it was less likely that ecclesiastical authority would surrender its claims to rational support or renounce its lordship over human intelligence. Faith might not need to lean on reason, but the title to this luxury along with other emoluments was still the right of the church. Thus the " natural " theology of Thomas, as well as the results of his harmonistic labors in placing the modern philosophy of that age at the disposal of Christian apologists, readily won official favor in spite of the Occamists' unquestionable loyalty to the authority of the church. It was the doctrinal system of Thomas that became the officially accepted dogma of the Catholic church at the Council of Trent in the sixteenth century. The papal bull of Pius IV, published on November 13, 1564, required all dignitaries and teachers of the church to swear allegiance to the pronouncements of the sacred canons and general councils, and particularly " the holy Council of Trent." The triumph of ecclesiastical authority over the entire area of doctrine was complete; the system as well as the person of Thomas had now been canonized.

LECTURE FOUR

◆ ◆ ◆
◆

BLAZING PATHWAYS TO FREEDOM

The medieval system of religious thinking, like the medieval cathedral, was constructed on a grand scale. Surveying this imposing product of their labors, orthodox divines unhesitatingly pronounced it very good. The church, with its clergy, its sacraments, its discipline and its dogma, represented the Deity authoritatively presiding over all of society's concerns. The laity, it was assumed, were incompetent to manage the affairs of a world hopelessly in bondage to Satan except as deliverance was mediated by the Catholic establishment. In principle, at least, all political, economic, religious, ethical and intellectual activities were subject to the will of the church.

To the casual observer at the opening of the fourteenth century it might have seemed that European civilization had now reached a state of permanent stability. No one any longer needed to feel uncertain about what men should believe or how they should act. The papacy stood ready to resolve all doubts or disagreements that might arise in any area of life pertaining to the affairs of either man or God. Notwithstanding many elements of diversity both in thinking and in action, an effective control seemed to have been established. Homogeneity had been secured by a generous policy of absorption or by an effectively superimposed authority. As yet discordant voices had been too few or too accidental to cause great anxiety. Older ways of thinking had been pursued to their logical outcome in the conception of a dominating ecclesiastical institution operating in accordance with well-defined interpretations of its rights and duties over the entire range of medieval life.

Appearances were, however, very deceptive. What seemed to be a peaceful triumph for the imperial church was only the calm preceding a storm of protest that was due to sweep over the medieval world with increasing fury in future centuries. The slumbering fires of discontent had not been extinguished; they were merely gathering strength for more disastrous eruptions. Dissatisfaction with the established order slowly but surely increased. The mounting spirit of nationalism threatened disaster to both political and ecclesiastical imperialism. Gradually men learned to think for themselves in a new way about the papacy and the church. Personal piety, rebelling against the external formalities of ritual and sacraments, sought a more satisfactory basis for religion within the depths of the soul. The laity, grown more confident of themselves, claimed the right to criticize, reform or abolish the privileged clerical class. As learning increased the individual demanded greater liberty of personal opinion. Bolder spirits began the often precarious task of blazing new paths to freedom of thought and action in the sphere of religion. The evolution of Christian doctrine slowly moved into a new phase.

I

One master-idea, although already grown decrepit, still cast its spell over Europe. This was the notion of the Holy

Roman Empire. It professed to perpetuate the ancient political glory of Rome transformed into a central European power closely linked with the papacy. In the struggle for supremacy between emperors and popes the latter had temporarily triumphed, but neither seems to have realized how empty the victory had been. While they both continued to appear in the picture, a third character intruded himself into the already confused scene. This was the king of the rising national governments, especially in France and in England. In the three-cornered conflict arising out of this complex situation, the doctrine of nationalism was destined to triumph over both ecclesiastical and political imperialism. This new trend did much to undermine the power of both emperor and pope in later medieval times.

The molding influence of the crusades on European thinking must also be taken into account. During the twelfth and thirteenth centuries this idealistic movement had resulted in the capture and then the loss of the Holy Land, but the after-effects continued to plague the minds of men for many a generation. Undoubtedly at the outset the crusading enterprise had augmented the prestige of the pope. He and his emissaries seemed to be the chief instigators and supporters of the holy war, and they pronounced the blessing of the church upon all who undertook to deliver the land of the Savior from bondage to the infidel. In theory at least the undertaking reflected glory on the papacy, even though in the course of time the control of the pope was completely eliminated. Thus he largely escaped blame for the ultimate failure of the long struggle, but the influences following in its wake could not be so easily dismissed.

One result fraught with disaster for the papacy was the increased power of the princes. Pope Urban II, in launching the first crusade, had vigorously admonished the warring nobles of Europe to cease internecine conflicts and unite to fight against the heathen in the East. The outcome had been the elimination from European society of many of the lesser warlords, while those who survived were able to advance more rapidly on the road to absolute monarchy. At the same time military efficiency had much improved with practice. Princes had acquired valuable experience in providing themselves with the sinews of war. They had learned how to collect taxes, train armies, encourage commerce, make treaties with powerful neighbors, and to build up the strength of their kingdoms. Once again the world had become military-minded. Respect for the sword had grown at the expense of excommunication and interdict, which were the pope's most powerful weapons. The total result was a great increase of national and monarchical sentiment constituting a formidable challenge to the authority of the papacy.

The doctrine of papal supremacy suffered a long series of reverses in its conflict with national sentiment during several centuries following the death of Boniface VIII in 1303. He had felt himself to be the very epitome of imperial power in both church and state. But barely two years after his death his successor removed the papal court to Avignon, where it remained more than seventy years subject to the will of the French monarchy. This fact alone was sufficient to shake the faith of other nationals, particularly when their kingdoms were at war with the French. Nor was the situation improved by the return of Pope Gregory XI to Rome in the year 1377. When he died the next year the so-called " Great Schism " followed, the Italians having a pope at Rome and the French one of their own at Avignon. The faithful were invited to pay court to one or the other of the two rivals. Quite naturally their national sympathies determined their choice, if indeed they did not spurn completely any notion of papal supremacy.

Thinking men do not contemplate with equanimity a threat of social chaos. They always strive to find some principle on which to build a program of integration. At the close of the thirteenth century the papacy had seemed to constitute the only unifying power capable of holding together in a measure of harmony the divergent elements of medieval life. A hundred years later this confidence had become badly shaken.

The growth of national diversities and the collapse of papal prestige inspired a quest for some more efficient medium of international expression. Two conceptions inherited from antiquity were available: the universal authority of the emperor and the decisions of a general council. Amid the confusion surrounding Dante in Italy in the opening decades of the fourteenth century he had voiced a passionate longing for the restoration of an imperial power like that of the old Romans under Augustus, a temporal ruler of the whole world who receives his authority directly from God rather than from the papacy. But contemporary emperors in the fourteenth and fifteenth centuries were far too narrowly proportioned to fit into the ancient mold. Flatterers might bedeck them with the imperial halo, but English and French kings and German princes were too powerful and too jealous of one another to permit the imperial figurehead to play so magnificent a role. Later the more learned and venturesome thinkers, like Marsilius of Padua in the early fourteenth century, and Jean Gerson a hundred years later, stoutly advocated a general council to effect, as it was phrased at the famous Council of Constance, a reformation of the church " in head and members," meaning the papacy and clergy.

The dignity of the emperor was somewhat rehabilitated by the new trend in thinking. According to tradition it had been the duty and privilege of an emperor to summon councils. At the outset the medieval advocates of conciliarism had not thought to pay any attention to this tradition. But the Council of Pisa in 1409, called by the authority of cardinals only, failed to effect desired reforms. It had elected a third pope without eliminating the two already in office. Not until the newly elected emperor, Sigismund, called the Council of Constance, which met in the autumn of 1414, was the papal schism brought to an end. Even so, it was neither the emperor nor the pope but the new national temper that emerged triumphant. For the Council had organized itself by " nations," following the custom in vogue at the universities, and had assigned one vote respectively to English, French, German and Italian groups. Before closing it had decreed that the pope should summon a like assembly after five years, and subsequently at regular intervals, to serve as a kind of parliament to watch over the activities of the papacy and the church. Thus popes, like kings, were confronted by an incipient national impulse to transform an absolute into a constitutional monarchy. While later popes successfully resisted the proposed restraints of conciliarism, they could not stem the rising tide of national resistance in lands beyond the Alps.

New economic trends also inspired resistance to papal supremacy. The medieval world, emerging from feudalism, gradually became money-minded. Popes, bishops, kings, merchants, craftsmen and peasants all learned to think in financial terms and concerned themselves, according to their several opportunities, with the acquisition of earthly as well as heavenly treasures.

From early times the Roman church had been enriched by the piety of the faithful. Already in the days of Gregory the Great the extensive " patrimony of St. Peter " yielded an enormous income over which Gregory exercised a diligent stewardship. In later years the estates of the church suffered severely from the depredations of the Lombards but were restored by the favor of the Franks, and in the course of time many new sources of income were established.

At an early date the pope's English subjects had voluntarily inaugurated the custom known as " Peter's pence," a contribution made by the king to support a " school of the Saxons " at Rome. This ultimately became a form of tribute paid with a fair measure of regularity until abolished by Henry VIII in the time of the English Reformation. Then there was the " Apostolic tax," paid annually by the monasteries and the princes of the various kingdoms to the pope as the feudal over-lord who insured to them the protection of heaven. Still another source of revenue was the "annates," so called because they represented the first year's income paid to Rome by the new incumbent of a benefice. Charges were also made for services rendered in connection with the nomination, consecration and confirmation of bishops and abbots. While in theory these fees were voluntary offerings, in practice they were as binding as the tips exacted in the European hotels in more recent times. Archbishops also paid a fee on receiving the pallium as the insignia of their allegiance to the pope. Bishops and abbots paid a "visitation" charge quite in excess of the amount necessary to defray the traveling expenses of the legates of the pope. He also demanded a share in the sums collected by bishops from the parish priests to whom they paid canonical visits. This too became a regular tax collected even when no visits were made.

The crusades furnished the popes a further opportunity to enlarge their income. They not only preached but also helped to finance this expensive undertaking. It was likewise a heavy drain upon the financial resources of the princes who now developed a new fiscal policy that perpetuates itself in the modern system of national taxation. They devised a levy called "tithes," imposed upon their subjects to defray the cost of the holy war. Since much of the property of each country was in the possession of churches and monasteries, these institutions were called upon to bear the greater part of the burden. The right of the secular authorities to tax religious holdings was naturally protested, especially by the pope, but he welcomed the suggestion of a new opportunity to repair his own finances. He did not propose to abolish tithes but claimed the sole right to control this revenue and sent his legates throughout Christendom to collect these moneys in addition to other papal incomes. The cessation of the crusades left the papacy thoroughly established in this new privilege, while the burdens of royal taxation were to be borne by the laity who were now the victims of both papal and monarchical greed.

Popes also laid claim to the estates of deceased bishops and threatened with excommunication any protesting relatives. Likewise revenues from vacant benefices flowed into the papal coffers. The more grasping pontiffs added to these incomes freewill offerings solicited from bishops and collected on pain of excommunication. In due course still other means were devised for extracting from laity and clergy, rich and poor, money to replenish the papal exchequer. One disinclined to observe the regular fasts could purchase the privilege of dining on meat, eggs and milk. One pledged to a crusade or to a laborious pilgrimage could obtain absolution for a monetary equivalent. Preachers were ordered to encourage even old men, women and children to obligate themselves to go on a crusade and then to avail themselves of the opportunity to purchase release. Thus the faithful added to their treasury of merit in heaven while the purse of the pope was filled with coins.

The sale of indulgences proved to be one of the most lucrative phases of papal finance. It was an old custom originating with bishops who had used it first to procure funds for the building of churches. In the time of the crusades it took on new vigor by becoming a distinctly papal instrument used to procure funds for all sorts of enterprises. One of the most notable instances was the sale of indulgences to finance the rebuilding of the basilica of St. Peter at Rome in the early sixteenth century. When the returns from Italy proved insufficient, the sale was extended to other European lands. In France, Spain and England the feeling of local independence had so far developed that national sentiment tended to supplant loyalty to Rome and thus to restrict the market for papal wares. But lack of national unity in Germany made it a more profitable field to cultivate. Here the pope's master-salesman, Tetzel, plied his trade until the pious monk, Luther, challenging the propriety of the pernicious business, struck the spark that lighted the fires of the Lutheran reformation.

Of course, at the outset Luther had no thought of abolishing the papacy or of altering radically the Catholic view of the church. His zeal was piously and practically motivated; it did not aim at establishing a new type of ecclesiasticism. Nor is it just to the Catholic church of that day to give Luther and his co-workers sole credit for perceiving and advocating the necessity of reforms. This desire had prompted the conciliar movement in the early fifteenth century, and in the middle of the sixteenth the Council of Trent substantially corrected abuses against which faithful Catholics had been continuously protesting for more than two hundred years. While a desire for reforms was widely current, it did not necessarily or generally imply a wish to break with the revered ecclesiastical institution. When the breach came it was only incidentally the outcome of religious idealism. Political and social forces were more immediately influential in shaping the course of events by which large numbers of Christians came to discover new paths of doctrine that no longer led to Rome. Kingdoms, principalities and communes were successfully blazing the way to autonomy in defiance of both an imperial pope and a Holy Roman emperor. Religion, when it chose to pursue the same course, found the route already prepared and protected by the secular authorities.

Every student of European history knows the familiar story. Without the patronage of the German princes, Luther could hardly have survived the condemnation of both pope and emperor. Otherwise his career would undoubtedly have ended as quickly and as disastrously as did that of John Huss a century earlier. Because German electors found it served their political ends, they were ready to adopt the programs of faith and order framed by Luther and Melanchthon and to make Lutheranism their state religion. Similarly, the establishment of local self-government in the Swiss cantons made possible the work of Zwingli at Zurich and Calvin at Geneva. In England even as early as the time of Wyclif patriotic and political considerations were already a menace to the authority of the papacy. It is perfectly apparent that Henry VIII was swayed fundamentally by national, political and economic interests in his dealings with the papacy that issued in the independent establishment of the English state church with the king as its supreme head on earth. Even the fiery religious zeal of John Knox in Scotland was so closely inter-woven with the struggle for national independence that the Scottish reformation often seems to have been primarily a political enterprise. Similar conditions marked the course of development in France, in the Netherlands and in the Scandinavian countries.

Out of this confusion a new doctrine regarding the ecclesi-astical establishment finally emerged. Henceforth the Prot-estant section of European Christendom rejected outright the notion of either papal or imperial supremacy. Church and state remained bound together, but the union was be-tween a specific territorial Christianity and the local civil or royal authority. Protestantism as a whole recognized no single head of the church on earth and devised no machinery for effecting institutional unity. The doctrine of national autonomy held for both church and state.

II

Having rejected the domination of the papacy, Protestant reformers were free to formulate a new interpretation of the church as an institution for engendering and ordering the religious life. But the immediate result was not so radical a change of doctrine as one might on first thought be led to expect. Of necessity hierarchical control was either aban-doned or given only a subordinate status, but denial of papal supremacy did not automatically abolish sacerdotalism and sacramentalism. These interests, having originated before the doctrine of papal authority arose, were quite capable of surviving its overthrow. Priests were functionaries of the local church and the ministration of the sacraments was a service rendered to the members of specific communities. Consequently, the reformers' break with the pope necessitated no essential change of attitude toward the traditional conception of the local church as a divine institution mediating salvation to a sin-cursed human race. The new way of thinking demanded only a rephrasing of ecclesiastical authority based on premises more fundamental to the immediate experiences and needs of the worshiper. Several different influences combined to determine the outcome.

There had been a notable resurgence of mysticism in the religious life of the later Middle Ages. Eckhart proclaimed that man possesses a divine faculty whereby he meets and communes with God on the supersensible plane of spiritual reality. This apprehension of deity was neither induced nor conditioned by any system of cult-mechanics; it was an immediate experience of the religiously responsive soul. Contemplation rather than either ritualistic observances or dogmatic speculations opened the door to the beatific vision. At the same time practical religious activities were emphatically demanded. One craved not merely a life of monkish solitude but, following in the footsteps of Christ, the believer devoted himself to the service of his fellow men. In the spirit of Francis of Assisi, Eckhart declared that " even were one in a rapture like Saint Paul, if he saw a sick man who needed his help it were much better that out of love he should abandon the rapture and serve the needy one in greater love."

Mystical piety assumed as its guiding principle direct access to Christ and to God on the part of every Christian. Eckhart affirmed that Christ was reborn in every pious soul. Thus one became a son of God, a truly deified person. By living under the immediate inspiration of deity and following the example set by Jesus, Christians in the present world completely attained to membership in the Kingdom of God. Alike for clergy and laity, disinterested love and altruistic service were the distinctive marks of devotion to the Kingdom. While as a rule the mystics meant no disloyalty to the Catholic establishment, their exaltation of the inner spiritual life above all externals, and their relative indifference to rewards based on " good works," represented an attitude tacitly hostile to all sacerdotalism, sacramentalism and religious legalism.

There were, to be sure, instances in which the rising tide of mystical piety and evangelical zeal broke through the dikes of established ecclesiasticism. Sometimes the breach was so slight as to be hardly perceptible. Although it resulted in the formation of new religious brotherhoods, like the " Brethren of the Common Life," and the " Friends of God," these societies were friendly substitutes for the church rather than its outspoken enemies. Their members were scarcely conscious of the extent to which they had departed from the existing system. In other quarters, where the severance was more deliberate and hostile, attempts were made to supplement criticism with a positive redefinition of the church and its authority.

In this connection one thinks immediately of Wyclif in England and Huss in Bohemia. While both were primarily involved in resisting the papacy, they and their followers undertook to revise current assumptions about the church. Reverting to Augustinianism, Wyclif declared that the membership of the true church consists only of those who have been predestined to salvation. The visible church, ministering sacraments and disciplining souls for heaven, is thus a secondary institution. The non-elect cannot have their status altered by means of sacerdotal rites, and for the elect the rites are unnecessary. Had this theory of the church — which was also advocated by Huss — prevailed, it would have annulled the entire sacramental and priestly system.

On the basis of strict logic Wyclif's theory made the visible church unnecessary for salvation. But membership in the Christian brotherhood, with its services of worship, its impressive ritual and its ethical codes inherited from the past, was accepted as divine ordinance and cherished for its practical value in nourishing the religious life. Those were still the days when it was universally assumed that everything of value in religion had to be substantiated by supernatural authority. When papal validity was called in question the mystic might satisfy his personal needs by resorting to inner experience, but his interpretation of experience required some sort of anchorage in historic revelation. If the contemporary ecclesiastical establishment seemed an insufficient divine agent, then God must have spoken more authoritatively to the revered Fathers of the church, or to the bishops assembled in ancient councils, or to his son Jesus Christ, or to the writers of the Scriptures. Both Wyclif and Huss sought in the Bible justification for their new doctrine of the church, a procedure in which they were followed by Luther, Calvin and other sixteenth century reformers. In fact, the substitution of Scriptural authority for that of the papacy ultimately became one of the most prominent features in all branches of Protestantism.

There was nothing essentially new in the Protestant disposition to affirm the authority of the Bible. The Catholics had always maintained its sanctity and desired that the laity should be made familiar with its precepts. Only when unauthorized preachers, like the Waldenses and the Cathari, used the Holy Book in support of heretical opinions, or to justify their resistance to the church, did the possession of the Scriptures by the laity incur the disapproval of the clergy. This was the motive that prompted the Council of Toulouse in the year 1229 to pronounce against vernacular translations and legislate that only the psalter and such portions of the Bible as were contained in the breviary should be given popular circulation.

Yet in spite of all official conservatism, knowledge of Scripture was more general in the later Middle Ages than has sometimes been supposed. Mystical piety drew its inspiration largely from this source. Loyal Catholics themselves freely used Scriptural texts to justify their demands for moral reforms within the church. Devout scholars among the humanists, and Erasmus in particular, revived the interest in antiquity and held up for admiration the original purity of Christianity depicted in the pages of the New Testament. The invention of printing and the extension of education accelerated the growth of interest in the Bible.

The admonition of Gregory the Great that everyone should read the sacred Scriptures daily had become the ideal of many pious souls. Even when they could not read Latin they had access to the Psalms and the Gospels in different vernacular renderings. Moreover, much of the popular devotional literature of the day, such as the widely read *Life of Christ* by Ludolph of Saxony, now current in several vernacular translations, was so rich in biblical quotations that one hardly needed a separate edition of the Scriptures. The reformers did not have to create a taste for the Scriptures but they found it exceedingly advantageous to their cause to cater to this awakening interest. And when they finally persuaded themselves and their followers to accept the Bible as the formal source of authority for church polity, ritual and dogma, they established a distinctly new way of thinking.

Although Protestants rejected papal dominion in favor of Scriptural authority and reconstructed the notion of the church largely in terms of individual religious living, they still carried forward substantial heritages from medieval Catholicism. The Christian life and the church as an institution were completely enveloped in an atmosphere of supernaturalism. The Lutheran doctrine of salvation by faith rather than works, and insistence on the priesthood of all believers, might seem to imply greater confidence in the ability of the individual to approach God directly and to order aright on man's own responsibility the affairs of the religious community. In practice Luther abundantly exhibited this capacity, but in principle he held exactly the opposite view. The same sense of fear for his soul's salvation that led him to abandon his prospects for a successful legal career and enter a monastery, drove him to further desperation as a monk striving to win his way to heaven by the arduous path of good works. He, like many other mystics, could not find full satisfaction in the penitential system. As an Augustinian he exalted God and abased men, not in the interests of a philosophical doctrine of the Absolute, which had so largely influenced Augustine's thinking, but as an escape from an overwhelming sense of human helplessness.

Even at the dawn of the sixteenth century fear and ignorance still reigned over wide areas of the common man's life. Devastating wars between rival princes and monarchs were always an imminent possibility. The Turks, now in possession of Constantinople, were a new menace to Christian Europe. The ambitious emperor was ever maneuvering to restore his waning prestige. Frequently would-be political and religious reformers had been unmercifully executed. The followers of Wyclif in England and of Huss in Bohemia had long been the objects of bloody persecution and the cruelties of the Inquisition had not yet been completely exhausted. But the ordinary individual found his enemies nearer at hand. Sanitation and social amelioration were unknown. Pestilence, famine and new diseases imported from the East were all too common. Overawed by man's apparent helplessness many persons sought asylum in the church where they expended such aggressive energies as they could muster on their own account in ascetic practices, veneration of relics, pilgrimages to shrines and monastic discipline. The age seemed to some Christians so utterly degenerate that they revived eschatological hopes and formed themselves into exclusive assemblies to await the early end of the world as the only practicable means of escape from the dominion of Antichrist.

There was, however, another level of medieval culture on which men moved with greater confidence in their own powers to understand and serve Deity. These Christians were the inheritors of the Renaissance which in the countries · north of the Alps revived ancient learning not merely for its own sake but for the help it could be made to render to contemporary life. The representatives of the movement were interested in religious, moral, political and social issues, and applied their acquisitions of learning to the strengthening of human energies for the solution of practical problems. They were concerned with what man had done and what he could do, while at the same time most of them were loyal to the Catholic church and entertained no thought of eliminating God from his place of primacy in the management of the world's affairs. These " humanists," as they are called, were ardent advocates of reform but they were not so frightened by the enormity of the task that they despaired of human efforts, nor were they so impatient that they were driven into open revolt against the existing ecclesiastical system. Neither Reuchlin, who gave Christian scholars of Europe their first dictionary of the Hebrew language, nor Erasmus, who prepared for them their first critical edition of the Greek New Testament, was able to feel at home in the Lutheran camp.

Luther, whose sympathies were with mystical piety rather

than with humanistic learning, had no notion of forming a new church wherein self-reliant individualism in religion could come to free expression. He believed as firmly as did the general run of Catholics that the ecclesiastical institution was absolutely necessary to the attainment of salvation. If external circumstances had not forced him outside the pale, probably he would have been content to carry on his work of reform strictly within the Catholic fold. He had found release from his personal fear of punishment for sin by magnifying the notion of the forgiving love of God revealed in Christ.

Here Luther was on common ground with the mystics, but they had not been so deeply impressed by the popular medieval dread of God's wrath. Hence for Luther salvation was completely realized when through faith the believer was fully reinstated in the good graces of deity. Thereafter the life of the Christian was one of perfect liberty; being free from all fear his salvation was accomplished without further need of penitential disciplines. Not even faith was to be accounted a work of merit, for when God had chosen to reveal his gracious love faith was an instinctive and involuntary response. It was the work of God, not of man. Thus Luther transformed his peculiar mystical experience into a specific doctrine of salvation that stood him in good stead when he was called upon to formulate a doctrine of the church wholly outside of the Catholic system.

Luther's church remained the sole ark of salvation because it was the only medium through which the forgiving love of God revealed in Jesus Christ became available. Salvation was effected by the proclamation of the gospel — the " Word of God " as Luther termed it. Of course, he had to dispense with the priestly hierarchy, but he did not derive knowledge of God solely from the reading of the Bible. In the light of the rigid biblicism later advocated by his followers he sometimes appeared dangerously radical. To call James " just a strawy epistle " seemed to be an unfortunate remark that had better be forgotten. While Luther believed that the sacred book contained the " Word," he also held that it was uttered in preaching and set forth in visible signs such as the rites of baptism and the Lord's Supper. By these means God's love was fully revealed; hence there was no need of any sacramentally mediated quantity of grace. When faith had been engendered by the hearing of the gospel the necessity for the priestly ministrations of the clergy disappeared. Since every believer thus became his own priest the old line of distinction between clergy and laity vanished. But the sacraments retained their validity by right of their revelatory significance. Thus without any sense of inconsistency Luther could still adhere to the Catholic dogma of transubstantiation.

Also the doctrine of the one true church was as dear to Protestants as to Catholics. Since the Catholic notion of a unity resident in the divinely instituted monarchical hierarchy was abandoned, some other integrating principle had to be discovered. This was located in the laity rather than in the clergy. At first Luther, following in the footsteps of Wyclif and Huss, identified the church universal with the totality of all those predestined to salvation, a view advocated still more vigorously by Zwingli and Calvin. But in Luther's thinking this invisible church later gave way to the more concrete reality of all true believers called by him the " community of saints " (*communio sanctorum*). This true church was essentially spiritual and universal. It was not to be identified with any specific ecclesiastical establishment or with any aggregation of multiple units. Yet it was composed of actual persons living upon earth and bound together by a common experience of saving faith and a united devotion to identical purposes. Luther specifically affirmed that " there is on earth, wide as the world is, not more than one holy general Christian church which is nothing else than the community or assembly of the saints."

While Protestants generally were agreed in resisting the suzerainty of Rome, they still adhered to the principle of ecclesiastical solidarity. Although they spoke of the invisibility of the true church, they constantly strove to make it concretely manifest on earth. Their prevailing conception is tersely expressed in the seventh article of the Augsburg Confession: "The church is the congregation of the saints in which the gospel is correctly taught and the sacraments correctly administered. And for the true unity of the church it is sufficient to agree concerning the doctrine of the gospel and the administration of the sacraments." Under more favorable circumstances the reformers would undoubtedly have organized a general council, as the Catholics had done a century earlier, to represent the notion of a united Christendom. But no such visible bond of unity was possible.

In different countries the local Protestant churches were

too dependent for their physical existence upon political and social conditions in their several territorial environments, and belief in the inseparability of church and state was as yet too binding, to permit Europe as a whole to organize an all-embracing Protestant establishment. A measure of solidarity within a politically unified territory was all that could be accomplished. This situation left the various groups of reformers in different countries free to work out independently their respective doctrines of the nature and function of their several communions. The result was a Protestantism itself divided into distinct branches characterized by diverse types of polity, belief and practice, as represented for example in the Lutheran, the Reformed, the Scottish and the English communions. Each branch maintained its ministry and its sacraments and formulated its creeds and confessions with as much assurance as Catholicism had ever displayed.

Protestants saw in their various establishments an authoritative institution divinely sanctioned for the purpose of effecting the salvation of human souls. They believed the church to be a foundation authorized by God, who had made provision for a legitimate ministry, a proper ritual, a valid creed and a distinctive type of polity. Thus their doctrine of the church was not so essentially novel as one might at first sight imagine. In comparison with many of the later medieval Catholic protests against externality and formalism in the life of the church, the institutional programs actually set up by different Protestant groups sometimes seem almost reactionary. Organized Protestantism gradually hardened into rigid systems of polity, ritual and dogma based on a

formal authority as binding as the theory of papal domination had ever been.   There arose also a Protestant scholasticism no less artificial and barren than that of medieval
Catholicism. Orthodox interpreters transformed the gospel
and primitive Christian tradition into a new law that shack-
led the spirits and minds of men with new chains that in
time became hardly less galling than the old had been. The
priesthood of all believers and the right of private judgment
in the interpretation of Scripture were indeed stressed by
the reformers in their conflict with Rome, but it is a gross
perversion of their position to infer that they advocated the
modern notion of absolute freedom for the individual in all
matters of religion, or that they envisaged a day to come
when every divergent group would be entirely free to organize itself according to its own liking into an independent
congregation.

Nevertheless the sixteenth century reformers deserve a
large measure of credit — or blame — for the growth of
ecclesiastical liberty that has marked the subsequent history
of Protestantism. Although its founders did not pursue
freedom's trail to its ultimate outcome, they established a
powerful precedent in favor of dissent. Diverging movements within Protestantism itself could not consistently be
denied the right of appeal to the principle of autonomy, from
which the life of the parent body had drawn its strength.
And in countries where the social sentiment was moving
irresistibly from monarchical to democratic ideals, and where
industrial, commercial and educational developments were
inviting the exercise of individual initiative, the church could

not remain static. The urge to change might be for better or for worse, but the urge could not be suppressed. The fundamental Protestant doctrine of liberty appeared to justify any proposed program that claimed to be a more accurate reproduction of the purity of the primitive church as disclosed in the Scriptures, the Fathers and the ancient creeds.

On the surface the appeal to antiquity might seem to be the primary motive for action, but in reality the more immediate incentive came from contemporary sensitivities of religious people and their awakening concern for spiritual and moral values. To free religion from bondage to external controls, whether of church or of state, to keep alive a vivid sense of personal piety while conforming to ritual and dogmatic prescriptions, to preserve a lively consciousness of immediate contact with God, to maintain the moral purity and spiritual vitality of church members on a level that would justify the title " community of saints " — these were recurring impulses that led to disputes about the doctrine of a true church and prompted renewed efforts at reforms resulting in the emergence of rival Protestant bodies.

The spirit of nonconformity was always more or less in evidence. From the start the various Protestant establishments had to reckon with one or another type of dissenting sect. The Anabaptists in Switzerland, the Socinians in Poland, the Arminians (Remonstrants) in Holland are well known separatist groups that in the sixteenth and seventeenth centuries maintained distinctive opinions about the nature and functions of the church and the essential characteristics of Christian life and doctrine. In England the

development of political institutions and the rise of the democratic temper produced much religious unrest, out of which
emerged various dissenting movements like Quakers, Puri-
tans, Presbyterians, Congregationalists, Baptists, Methodists.
And in the English settlements in America, where Old
World restraints were relatively weak, and where democratic procedures and individual freedom became highly
idealized, the disposition among Protestants to multiply rival
religious organizations found extravagant expression. The
doctrine of institutional liberty became a kind of denominational license used to justify an excessive and wasteful
competition between numerous mutually antagonistic Protestant groups.

III

In spite of their conservatism the reformers were doughty
champions of liberty. They pointed the way to new paths
of thinking that freed Christianity from bondage to the
papal hierarchy, restored to the laity equality of rights with
the clergy, and liberated the religious life from subservience
to ritualistic formalities and mechanically operating sacraments. The measure of this service was so great that one
hesitates to comment upon other aspects of the reformers'
work pointing in an opposite direction. They not only
failed to blaze a new highway for the exercise of intellectual
freedom in the interpretation of theological doctrines, but
they insisted even more rigidly than did many of their
Catholic contemporaries upon submission to orthodox tradition in dogma, and they uncompromisingly demanded strict

adherence to ancient authorities in all matters of belief. In this respect they were reactionary propagandists for authoritarianism rather than prophetic heralds of freedom in religious thinking.

This role was deliberately chosen by the reformers, and in the light of their situation the choice seemed amply justified. As they viewed the state of affairs, the church was functioning inadequately in their world, not because men were making new demands upon religion, but because the church had lost its supposed original efficiency. Present-day modernists are wont to envisage a quite different type of task. Their problem is so to refashion organized religion that it can be made to meet adequately conditions by which it has never before been confronted. As the world changes, the church, it is assumed, also needs to change. But the sixteenth-century reformers worked from a very different hypothesis. Conceiving the church in its original purity to have been designed by God to be a perfect instrument for all time to come, they saw in its contemporary failures only an evidence of deterioration. Consequently their task was to restore it to its primitive state of perfection. All of their reasoning proceeded from this major premise.

Subsidiary interests also affected the thinking of the reformers. Being in the minority they were always on the defensive. Certainly they were not lacking in intellectual vigor, but they were forced to expend their mental energy largely in apologetic efforts. As restorers of old truth, rather than discoverers or creators of new doctrine, it was incumbent upon them to demonstrate the validity of their teaching by reference to authentic ancient models. Novelties were necessarily taboo. Melanchthon, the first systematic theologian of Lutheranism, explicitly affirmed: " We have introduced no new dogma into the church, but we renew and illustrate the doctrine of the Catholic Church." This truth was to be found fully embodied in the Scripture and comprehended in the Apostles', the Nicene, and the Athanasian creeds.

The system of Protestant dogma elaborated by Melanchthon, Zwingli, Calvin, and their followers need not be described in detail at the present moment. One who is not already familiar with its content may easily acquire the desired information from abundant literature on the subject. Except for its views on ecclesiology and sacerdotalism, Protestantism was essentially medieval in both spirit and substance. Its estimate of human beings and their native mental and spiritual powers was exceedingly pessimistic. The liberty claimed for the laity did not mean greater confidence in the religious capacities of the ordinary man. Worthy religious attainments were beyond his reach, save as he became the recipient of totally unmerited favors from God. The biblical account of Adam's fall was determinative for all orthodox Protestant anthropology. " Man," said Calvin, " is utterly corrupt and depraved and humility alone becomes him in the presence of God, who is all that man is not."

Such virtues as Christians possessed were in the nature of a divine donation and when exercised aright yielded undeviating obedience to God's will as revealed in ancient times. The end of all effort was strict conformity to the divine commands, not because these were adjudged by man to be inherently good but because they were the decrees of heaven. Natural reason was assigned an important function, particularly by Melanchthon, Zwingli and Calvin, who carried over a large heritage from contemporary humanism, but reason when legitimately employed always followed in the footsteps of revelation. Thus theology became a strenuous intellectual enterprise directed toward the understanding and exposition of revelation. The result was a Protestant scholasticism that rivaled the technique of Thomas Aquinas and issued in a dogmatic rigidity and an adherence to creedal formulas as binding as anything Catholicism had ever produced. One must look to other sources than the Protestant reformation for the earliest encouragement of intellectual freedom in the shaping of religious beliefs and the liberation of the human mind from bondage to ecclesiastical dogma.

The intellectual ferment that had been set in motion by the Renaissance was perpetuated in the humanists' concern for the revival of learning. But the movement had suffered a distinct setback as the problem of religious authority forced itself into the forefront of attention in the sixteenth century. Both the Protestant reformation and the so-called " counterreformation " of the Catholics stressed anew the necessity of submission to an external law of belief and practice. Each cause invited intellectual supporters, who directed their mental energies toward defending the views of the party whose interests they sought to serve. Scholarship was subordinated to apologetic demands. Thus the new learning, drafted into the service of the church, found itself no longer

master of its own domains. It was subject not only to the
official creeds of the church but also to the civil authorities
that either controlled the church or did its bidding. The
Protestants when in power were no less insistent than the
Catholics upon the duty of the government to persecute
heretics and non-conformists. Intellectualism had, as it were,
to begin afresh the task of discovering new pathways to
freedom. We must be content for the moment to sketch in
mere outline the growth of this movement under the impact
of new forces that affected more particularly the thinking of
Protestants.

Men of mental vigor are pretty sure to think well of their
intellectual efforts. They may, like Augustine, take pride in
reasoning their way to a doctrine of human insignificance;
or they may, with Descartes, find in their thought-processes
the ultimate ground of reality. The latter tendency grew
in strength throughout the seventeenth century. Reason
and conscience in the individual increasingly asserted their
rights over against the superimposed authority of both
church and state. Among the countries of Europe, Holland
presented a political situation that allowed the largest measure of liberty of opinion. There several radical sects had
already found a congenial home. The Anabaptists were
preaching a complete separation between the civil and the
spiritual order, freedom of conscience for the individual, and
man's personal responsibility for keeping the law of God.
They, like the Remonstrants (Arminians), stoutly resisted
the Calvinistic emphasis on divine predestination. This resistance was further strengthened by the Socinians who,

when inconvenienced by Jesuit pressure in Poland, found a more comfortable environment in Holland. They stoutly defended the native power and ability of man to choose and pursue the way of virtue and to judge the validity of doctrine in the light of human reason. They prized the divine enlightenment from above revealed in the Holy Scriptures, but they refused to concede that revelation contained anything contrary to right reason.

The relatively tolerant atmosphere of Holland invited numerous refugees — both new religious societies and restless individuals — who found there freedom to develop interests close to their hearts. There it was that Descartes, originally a French Jesuit, worked out his widely influential rational philosophy. There too, Spinoza, whose ancestors had escaped the persecution of the Jews in Spain, made his home. The liberal Pierre Bayle, driven from France by hostility to the Huguenots, resided in Amsterdam where he published his notable *Philosophical Dictionary*. Similarly the English philosopher, John Locke, while living as a fugitive in Holland, wrote his memorable little treatise, *The Reasonableness of Christianity as Delivered in the Scriptures*. Without multiplying illustrations one easily perceives that powerful trends toward intellectual freedom were demanding recognition within European culture during the seventeenth century. These tendencies were evident as yet only on the periphery of the church, so to speak, but their trend was perfectly apparent. They were moving away from the traditional Protestant emphasis on supernaturalism to a rational and natural basis in religion; and from the notion of man's total depravity, helplessness and volitional futility to confidence in his powers of choice, strength of mind and ability to judge for himself in the affairs of religion.

After the Act of Toleration in 1689 England offered a more attractive setting for freedom of thinking. Respect for man and nature rapidly increased despite all ecclesiastical dogma to the contrary. As in the second and third centuries, once again Christianity's need for maintaining intellectual respectability compelled adjustments to current philosophical developments. Reason claimed sovereignty over religious opinions. An increasing number of loyal churchmen, or near-churchmen, welcomed the new master as a benefactor to the Christian cause. The result was the course of intellectual history familiarly associated with such terms as Rationalism, Deism and the Enlightenment. It was an interesting development, revealing many variations in detail, but its general result was the insistent application of reason to all religious questions.

Rational theology was quite as authoritarian in its own way as traditional dogma had ever been. Reason was something that transcended this or that individual mind and was supposed to possess the same quality of inerrancy that had commonly been ascribed to revelation. All men who thought properly would, it was assumed, arrive at identical conclusions. A hypothetical rational order inhering in nature seemed to insure the normative quality of all true thinking. Respect for natural law had been much enhanced by the scientific observations of Kepler, Francis Bacon, Newton and others. Thus natural theology, formerly pursued by the scholastics to support and clarify revelation, gradually assumed the role of dictator. Reason presumed to furnish the key to all true religious knowledge and to give rules for the guidance of all moral conduct.

Being the modernists of their day, the rationalist theologians attempted to do full justice to current intellectualism and at the same time maintain unimpaired the values of traditional religion. The older apologetic based on Scriptural revelation, the fulfillment of prophecy and proof from miracles, had now to be either rehabilitated or discarded. Rehabilitation was the program most widely adopted by the early rationalists. They were inclined to make religion a rather tightly knit philosophical system whose truth could be adequately demonstrated by the human mind. But not all men, either in ancient or modern times, were thought intellectually capable of comprehending the truth and obeying the precepts of natural religion. Consequently revelation had been added in order to establish religious duties and promote virtue. The divine character of Christianity had been revealed in the fulfillment of ancient prophecies, in the advent of Jesus as Messiah, in the miracles attending the founding of the new religion, in the moral demands of Christian teaching, and in the disclosure of future rewards and punishments. All of these things were believed to be strictly in harmony with the findings of natural reason. One trusted in the supernatural because its testimony was capable of rational defense. Thus the older type of apologetic was thrown into reverse.

Not all rationalists were willing to dismount at this half-way station of thought. If supernatural intervention served only the practical purpose of inculcating virtue, but was no essential addition to philosophic truth, might it not be utterly discarded? The Deists, as they are called, advanced to this position. They agreed with their fellow rationalists in exalting reason but doubted the supplementary worth of revelation. Everything contributing to virtue could, they believed, be known most accurately by reason and in no other way. The moral perfection of God was rationally demonstrable and the goal of all worth-while religion was man's apprehension and imitation of God's virtues in the interests of both individual and public good. Arguments from prophecy and miracle seemed unworthy of a truly enlightened mind and liable to be a detriment rather than an advantage to the most worthy type of morality, in which for these thinkers religion principally consisted.

The modernist is always tempted to oversimplify his problem by eliminating from consideration things that to him are uncongenial or unimportant, and then positing finality for his conclusions. In his efforts to conserve the values of tradition he also tends to ignore historical perspective by making the past a mere replica of the present. When he has thus re-read history he too discovers therein a static norm valid for all time. Many apologists for Christianity in the eighteenth century were the victims of this delusion. They reduced religion to a body of coldly rational dogma and ethics, normative because in alleged agreement with natural reason, to which they appended traditional belief in supernaturalism revised in harmony with their particular philosophical views. This mediating procedure, although well-intentioned, gave offense to both liberals and conservatives. The former sought a still larger freedom for thinking more vitally connected with the new experiences of a modern age, and the latter demanded more room for the cultivation of emotional warmth in spiritual affairs. Life in the various European countries at the close of the eighteenth century was already far too complex to permit all intellectual and religious interests to be cast into the narrow mold of an authoritarian rationalism.

LECTURE FIVE

CROSSROADS IN THE MODERN SCENE

At the close of the eighteenth century the dawn of a new age of liberalism in religion was beginning to break over the entire Protestant world. After a long and checkered history the principle of toleration had widely triumphed. In the chief countries of northern Europe the government retained jurisdiction over religious affairs, recognizing one or another communion as the official church of the state, but it no longer undertook to suppress all other branches of Christendom. Even the smaller sects, if free from the taint of political suspicion, were generally conceded the right of assembly and enjoyed greater freedom in the conduct of their internal affairs than was sometimes true of the state church.

In matters of belief the attitude of the governments was also tolerant. In the main, individuals were accorded full liberty of conscience. They were free to follow personal taste in the choice of a religious fellowship and in the phrasing of their doctrinal tenets. Even when they were adherents of a state church, which always had its official creed, loyalty to the institution did not necessarily mean strict assent to every item in the traditional formulas of the church, any more than loyalty to the state required absolute uniformity of political opinions among all citizens. When creedal restraints were imposed, the ecclesiastical rather than the civil authorities were likely to be the chief instigators of intolerance.

Among the various independent churches, especially in America where the principle of separation was now universally operative, all communions enjoyed equal rights and were entirely free from interference by secular authorities. Each denomination was autonomous in all respects, a situation that in a measure militated against the religious freedom of the individual. Since the various denominations were disposed to require strict adherence to a creed, the intellectually alert individual who deviated from the prescribed doctrine of his communion was liable to trial for heresy before an ecclesiastical court. While the state refused to cast him into prison or burn him alive at the behest of his co-religionists, they could impose other forms of punishment from which his only escape was either abandonment of organized religious activity or the gathering of a few like-minded persons to form a new denomination.

Thus religious liberty, increasingly conferred upon Protestants by the democratic type of social organization emerging in different countries, introduced much variety into the form and content of Christian doctrines. Separate communions advocated one or another type of dogma, usually claiming in each instance divine authority for their creedal pronouncements. Not infrequently one would find in their several systems of dogma striking divergences if not outright contradictions even in essential matters like notions about the nature of the church and its ministry, the validity of the Scriptures as revelation, the natural man's status before God, the person of Christ, the scheme of salvation, the character of the Deity, the relation between morals and religion, and other topics usually included in a system of dogma.

Within society today the most traditionally conservative ways of thinking are found flourishing side by side with the most modern and liberal, with all sorts of variations occupying the intervening territory. In the absence of a central ecclesiastical or political authority to decree a uniform course for the Protestant mind to pursue, its peregrinations have become erratic and confusing. One who attempts to discover the chief highway over which Protestant doctrine is moving today finds the task exceedingly difficult. The landscape is traversed by a perplexing network of crossroads, each bidding for the traffic and alleged by its admirers to be the main thoroughfare. It may help to clarify the situation if we survey the factors that have contributed most directly to produce this state of uncertainty.

I

Eighteenth-century rationalism had done much to clear the way for the coming of nineteenth-century liberalism. The rationalists developed the optimistic thesis that man is so thoroughly reasonable as to be able to order his individual and corporate existence in a way that will exalt benevolent above selfish impulses and realize the largest possible measure of justice, equity, happiness and spiritual excellence within human society. This assumption placed a heavy burden of responsibility upon human nature. But the procedure did not seem absurd, since man's rational faculty was assumed to be virtually a divine mind. The presupposition was the same whether held by a loyal churchman who believed the ecclesiastical establishment to be a divine institution because rationally defensible, or by a deistic anti-churchman like Voltaire or the author of the *Age of Reason*. In either case humanity was thought capable of accomplishing its own salvation. If it needed divine assistance it discovered the will and ways of God by the exercise of its intellectual powers, or if it felt no such need it might proceed successfully without benefit of clergy to usher in Utopia. The hope of the world lay in the free operation of a utilitarian intellectualism, whether within or without the church. This attitude was widely prevalent among the intelligentsia, particularly in England, during the latter part of the eighteenth century.

Meanwhile a strong counter current had set in. Rationalism had virtually deified reason. Displays of enthusiasm or any other forms of irrational motivation were sharply discountenanced. At the same time life was becoming more complex, the imaginations of men were being stimulated by broadening contacts, and exclusive concentration upon the inner world of the mind began to give way to a multiplicity of stimuli impinging upon the individual from without. An accumulating mass of varied human experience demanded recognition. The industrial revolution in England had already begun. The transition from rural to urban conditions, the invention of machinery, the expansion of commerce, the rise of the competitive system with consequences both happy and distressing for the individual, all contributed towards the stimulation of feeling. Respect for human emotions, outgrowing the limited domains of reason, embraced within the scope of liberty an individual's title to cherish desires, aspirations and possessions for his personal satisfaction. It began to be believed that all men should be privileged to think and act in line with their tastes. They were sentient as well as rational beings, and perhaps more fundamentally sentient than rational. It was inevitable that the supremacy of reason in both philosophy and religion should be challenged by a heightened regard for experience and feeling.

In the realm of philosophy Hume voiced most clearly the temper of the newly awakening empiricism. A century earlier Locke, indeed, had made sense-perception the basis of all knowledge, but he had then proceeded to subject the data of experience to the mental processes of a strict rationalism. Hume, on the other hand, made all human convictions in the last analysis a product of sensations organized in response to the desire to realize pleasure and avoid pain. Reason was thus only a tranquillity of mind arrived at by one's transcending discordant emotions and attaining to a state of immediate satisfaction in feeling. This was a thoroughgoing empiricism that cut the ground completely from under optimistic rationalism. It freed the individual from the rigid authority of reason but made him the helpless victim of his hopes and fears, pleasures and pains, joys and sorrows. Undoubtedly this was a state of mind widely experienced at the moment by the populace even though they may have known little and cared less about the philosophical system offered for its justification.

An empirical view of life liberated the human spirit from the restraints of an artificial rationalism but left it at the mercy of the sterner realities of immediate experience. Less hardy minded persons, realizing the helplessness of the natural man, turned eagerly again to supernaturalism. If God did not speak clearly through man's reason, then one must have recourse to the supernatural manifestations of the divine mind, especially as revealed in the Scriptural records of the miraculous. Hume, on applying the empirical test of truth to miracles, found them wanting. He did not deny their possibility but he questioned the adequacy of human testimony to prove their authenticity in so indubitable a fashion as to make them safe ground for religious confidence. Paley's reply on behalf of the orthodox rationalists seemed to many of his contemporaries a sufficient refutation of all doubts, but the attempt actually forced the Christian apologist to accept a semi-empiricism. His most potent argument was to the effect that miracles are to be believed because they are needed to support the idea of revelation.

From this feeling of need later defenders of the faith moved on to still more subjective arguments based on a sense of the divine character of Christianity. Since one felt that this religion contained within itself divine values, it seemed proper to suppose that its truth would be attested by supernatural displays, especially in connection with its establishment. When the experienced worth of the Christian religion was made to support belief in miracles, the pattern was set for a type of thinking widely in vogue throughout the nineteenth century and current even down to the present time. In the last resort personal conviction regarding the worthy character of Christianity became the measure of religious truth.

Another type of anti-rational protest arising in eighteenth-century England has also left a lasting impression upon Protestant thinking, particularly in England and America. This was the evangelical movement, with which the name of John Wesley is most conspicuously associated. Its keynote was subjective religious experience supplemented by a methodical discipline in the devotional life. It derived its first impulse from German pietism mediated by a small Moravian community assembled in London, but it soon developed distinctive characteristics under the vigorous leadership of Wesley and his associates. The protest against rationalism was practically rather than philosophically justified, and primacy was given to the assurances of feeling in religion. Traditional items of belief, slurred over or explained away by the rationalists as distasteful to intelligent persons, were now elevated to the position of first importance. The followers of Wesley reaffirmed the total depravity of man, the utter worthlessness of mere human morality and intellectualism, belief in the trinity and in the strictly supernatural character of salvation, the immediacy of guidance by the Holy Spirit, the necessity of faith based on inner vision rather than on reasoned arguments, the other-worldliness and perfection of the Christian life, the binding authority of Scriptural revelation, and the rejection of all views about the universe that did not harmonize literally with the statements of the Bible.

Doctrinally, English evangelicalism represented a wholesale reversion to medieval ways of thinking perpetuated in earlier Protestantism. But in their emphasis on practical activities the disciples of Wesley showed themselves much more sensitive than orthodox rationalists had been to the popular religious needs of the contemporary age. Although the natural man was totally helpless, the redeemed man bore a heavy responsibility for making a better world. Wesley himself had shied away from the Calvinistic doctrine of the absolute divine sovereignty, and the consequent stress on predestination, lest the volitional energy of man be so weakened as to make him indifferent to his personal obligations. More recently an effort has been made to show that Wesley was a good Calvinist, but he seemed a dangerous Arminian to his Calvinistic contemporary, Whitefield. While the two leaders disagreed on this subject, the question was really a philosophical issue not essentially important to either of them. At heart they were both incurable activists who necessarily assumed that man was to labor indefatigably for the salvation of the world irrespective of one or another philosophical theory. Doctrinal consistency was of less moment than effective religious living inspired by one's personal experience of spiritual realities. Thus the Wesleyan movement was not only a protest against narrow rationalistic intellectualism but was also a stimulus to spontaneous individualism, particularly in the realm of the emotions.

The reinstatement of the feelings in religion also promoted in a practical way the essential principles of empiricism. Hume and Wesley never could have agreed in their attitude toward miracles, but in some respects they had much more in common than either of them realized. They were fundamentally one in deriving knowledge from subjective experience, in making emotional satisfaction the ultimate test of convictions, in freeing the individual from an externally imposed law of reason, and in paving the way for a program of action in which man assumed direct responsibility for advancing human welfare. In a soil thus prepared ideals of Christian social service and reform germinated and came to remarkable expression in the nineteenth century.

In Germany at the opening of the nineteenth century intellectualism showed a slightly different trend from that in England, although the note of self-assurance was no less pronounced. A hundred years earlier Leibnitz, whom we may credit with having inaugurated the Enlightenment in Germany, had assigned a new importance to the individual by asserting that individuality envelops the infinite within itself. This idea furnished the basis for a highly optimistic view of life. Progress was insured by the self-development of personality. Human reason, being grounded in the divine reason as it came to expression through the process of education, guaranteed a gradual improvement in human conditions. Religion and philosophy were phases of a single rational order gradually evolving toward a happier state as the perfection of God became ever more completely manifested in the moral and religious life of humanity. Religion was essentially an affair of the spirit, and the enlightenment — one might say the self-enlightenment — of Christian men was its noblest display. From this premise Leibnitz deduced his doctrine of an inevitable evolution upwards and a belief in historical progress.

Leibnitz's hopeful view of human society was purely idealistic, a grand vision corresponding to no reality in the contemporary life of the German people. While they enjoyed a large measure of religious freedom they had no sense of social and political unity such as then obtained in France and England. Religious toleration and denominational parity had been secured to the Lutheran, the Reformed and the Catholic churches in German territory by the Treaty of Westphalia that closed the Thirty Years' War in 1648; but German Christians, even Protestants, possessed no central ecclesiastical institution. Political unification was still more remote. Different territorial princes maintained themselves as best they could against the aggressions of one another and against the imperial ambition of Austrian claimants to sovereignty over the German states. The once thriving Hanseatic League, that had brought about a measure of industrial and commercial unity, had been completely wrecked by the Thirty Years' War. From this disaster Germany's economic power showed only feeble signs of recovery until the establishment of the " Tariff Union " (*Zollverein*) in 1834. For a long time foreign interference, from England, France and Russia, had been a serious deterrent to the rise of nationalism, and the Napoleonic wars still further retarded the unification of Germany.

These circumstances exerted a distinct influence upon the trend of thinking represented by the German Enlightenment. At the outset its sponsors had derived their intellectual stimuli largely from other countries, and their thinking was not closely integrated with the disrupted state of society in Germany. Thus they were free to develop their interest in ideas, without the measure of immediate reference to the established institutions of church or state that often influenced English or French rationalists. Individualism and idealism were not compelled to become practical and therefore did not experience the restraints that otherwise might have inhibited free intellectual pursuits. German thinkers devoted themselves more particularly to the inner world of ideas wherein they won unique distinction.

Reason was later in asserting its triumph in Germany than in England, but the results were more significant for the development of Christian doctrine in the nineteenth century. Leibnitz had been so far in advance of his age that after his death his views on the universal validity of reason in the individual and in history remained virtually dormant for nearly a century until revived and recast by Lessing. Only at the close of the eighteenth century and in the early years of the nineteenth did the intellectual vigor of the German Enlightenment come to maturity and then in a distinctive form, as represented particularly in the philosophies of Kant and of Hegel. While they were ardent disciples of reason, they were a long way removed from the older form of rationalism that had flowered in England. The pragmatic moralism of Kant and the absolute idealism of Hegel introduced into religion conceptions determinative for much subsequent thinking and still substantially reproduced in certain widely popular types of present-day Christian doctrine.

The reaction against rationalism in Germany took a somewhat different course both philosophically and religiously from that followed in England. The German pietistic awakening that preceded the Enlightenment had arisen on the ruins of the social order following the disastrous Thirty Years' War. Theologically, it was a revolt against a barren Protestant scholasticism before rationalism had appeared upon the scene. It was a protest against formality in doctrine and practice rather than a deliberate effort, as was the case in the Wesleyan movement, to restore orthodox beliefs. While its doctrines were thoroughly traditional — even medieval — in content and form, its spirit was one of liberation rather than reaction and tended to free the individual from the grip of a creedal and sacramental institutionalism. In its efforts to renew the spiritual life of the inner man it depended less upon the methods of emotional revivalism than upon devotional study of the Bible, cultivation of the prayer-life and mutual edification of believers. Although the natural man and human society were viewed pessimistically, and an ascetic ideal almost monastic in its protest against worldliness in the church was inculcated, the pietists were devoted to the service of their fellow men. They were active in educational work, they ministered to the poor and established asylums for orphans, and the memory of their zeal for missionary work in heathen lands survives even to the present day.

Thanks largely to the earlier work of the pietists, when the German intellectual movement in religion arose it could not proceed independently of inner spiritual realities already deeply rooted in a very influential section of Protestantism. The rights of feeling, soberly harnessed to the practical activities of religion and freed from subservience to dogmatic and ritual formalities, had become firmly entrenched. Here were data that even imperial reason could not ignore. Kant's categorical imperative, though derived from practical reason, was at bottom a subjective feeling of moral obligation that supplied the point of departure for his rational interpretation of religion. Hegel, too, found in feeling the genesis of the religious consciousness which, when disciplined by reason, yielded a complete system of Christian doctrine based on the capacity of the finite to sense the infinite and on the ability of the human mind to read in nature and in history the self-revealing presence of the idealistic absolute.

Schleiermacher gave religious feeling a new dignity. Evidently he was much influenced by the pietists, as well as by the romantic tendency with its poetic urge to free the individual from enslavement to the exigencies of an unhappy social environment and permit him to revel in the simplicity of an idealized state of nature. Rousseau's extravagant naturalism, that played so significant a role in French thinking, acquired a measure of sobriety in the romanticism of Herder, Goethe and other German exponents, but it retained its native appreciation of the immediacy of feeling and its high regard for a fresh and ebullient quality of life that inspired confidence in the natural powers of the individual and in the optimistic view of the historical process.

Yet Schleiermacher did not go all the way with either the pietists or the romanticists. He could not follow the former in their disposition to assign normative authority to dogma and ethical codes. The essential thing in religion, its abiding and unchanging reality, was the feeling of unity with the infinite. Thinking and action were not to be divorced from religion; they were its accidents, one might say its natural fruits, and varied according to circumstances. Religion, on the other hand, was at heart an unchanging reality rooted in a subjective experience that entitled it to an independent dignity and esteem.

At the same time there was in Schleiermacher a strain of rationalism that differentiated his thinking from that of the romanticists. He could not follow through to the end their relativism and excessive naturalism, which seemed to him to involve an improper subordination of religion to culture. He likewise refused to enslave religion to either philosophy or science. Although he made religion virtually an idealized emotion, he would not allow that it was a system of idealized knowledge. His contemporary, Hegel, provided a place in philosophy for feeling but assigned it no religious content; it was only the point of departure for a rational process leading to knowledge of the infinite. Schleiermacher, however, found in feeling itself the only dependable bond of union with the infinite. This subjective certainty was the essential and ultimate reality for all religion.

Such was the rich and varied heritage with which nineteenth-century liberalism started. The fetters of medieval scholastic dogma, even as perpetuated in Protestantism, had been shaken off by modernists of the rational temper. A few of them went to the logical extreme of denying outright the validity of all Christian tradition in favor of a purely natural religion, or of no religion at all. But the majority among the intellectuals remained loyal to Christianity and propounded a type of thinking that has not inappropriately been termed a natural supernaturalism. Others moved more congenially in the realm of inner ideas, where they found their yearning for connection with the infinite better satisfied by recourse to moral and philosophical idealism. While still others, rebelling against the absolutism of intellectual tyranny, reaffirmed the rights of the feelings in religion, either reverting to the traditional notion of a supernaturally instigated emotionalism or a more natural type capable of commanding intellectual respect. In the latter event religious feeling acquired an independent status and claimed separate recognition side by side with the data of philosophy and science. But more empirical and positivistic modes of procedure, dealing primarily with the reality of observable phenomena and the construction of a better way of life in terms of concrete human relations, had not yet attained wide recognition in the shaping of Christian doctrines. These aspects of liberalism still awaited development.

II

During the latter half of the nineteenth century Protestant doctrine moved with increasing self-assurance along the highway of liberalism. The age was one of rapid expansion over a wide range of activities in various Protestant countries. Germany effected national unification under the leadership of Prussia. The American people spread westward to the Pacific and attained a new sense of solidarity following the Civil War over the question of slavery. England built up her colonial empire. The inhabitants of widely separated territories, becoming more acutely aware of one another's existence, sensed the unity of all civilization. Racial and national isolation gave way to a new concern for internationalism. By means of treaties between rival powers and the establishment of an international peace conference that first met at The Hague in 1899, the Utopian hope of a world peace seemed to be within the grasp of civilized man.

Very significant social developments were also in evidence. Industry and commerce made long strides ahead in various countries, while trade between nations welded the different peoples of the earth together in a complicated network of economic relations. At the same time democratic sentiment increased and individual initiative was stimulated. The rapid development of machinery and the factory system of production not only made labor class-conscious but augmented the growth of capitalism. As social relations became more intricate, the solution of social problems grew more difficult. But even in this area of interest no single community or nation lived entirely to itself. Questions about human welfare and the betterment of social conditions were discussed in the light of events and conditions obtaining in different parts of the world.

Cultural developments also became a more common possession. Learning took on a cosmopolitan character as the literary productions of one country were translated into the language of other peoples, and students from different parts of the world went abroad to attend universities in foreign lands. Education acquired a new dignity and attracted more general attention. The results of study and research affected popular thinking and action over wider and wider areas of life. A college or a university training came to be thought necessary for success not only in a professional career but even in business or politics. One might almost say that the whole world went to school. Everyone knew, or assumed that he could know, something about everything. At any rate the individual felt entitled to entertain personal opinions on a wide range of subjects, including even religion. On the other hand, if he feared the Scylla of dilettantism he might be caught in the whirlpool of a narrow specialization where he lost all sense of the unity of knowledge. If, for instance, he were a physical scientist, he might spurn all religious ideas; or if he were a theologian his metaphysical gyrations might utterly blind him to the significance of physical and social facts in the area of religion.

Developments within Protestantism during this period were closely bound up with the process of political, social and cultural growth, especially in the British Empire, Germany and the United States. An ever increasing number of religious thinkers caught the spirit of the times. They broadened the range of their interests to include subject-matter and points of view that formerly would have seemed unworthy of a theologian's attention. Religious thinking had now to reckon with new types of philosophical speculation, changed standards for measuring the dependability of knowledge, a physical world growing incomprehensibly vast in its expanse, a greatly elongated view of the duration of the historical process, more exacting methods for testing the data of history, radically altered notions about the physical and mental constitution of man, and new insights into the structure of human society. A babel of voices clamored at the doors of the cloister or the lecture room, forcing theologians to heed more generously the call of the multitude. The once majestic self-crowned " queen of the sciences " had to descend from her throne to walk the streets in contact with all kinds of people and ideas.

The general trend in the new type of theological thinking was marked by a movement away from exclusive concern with the inner world of feeling and mind to the outer world of physical and social reality. Historical study became a very influential factor in determining the course of doctrine. Hegelian philosophy of history supplied the point of departure for the new venture launched by the well-known Tübingen School of biblical criticism in the thirties of the nineteenth century. Under the scrutiny of F. C. Baur and his successors the New Testament literature no longer remained a permanent deposit of literal truth. Rather, it represented an evolutionary process in the conflict of religious ideas to free the human spirit from bondage to the letter of Scripture — the outward symbols of religion — in order that it might discover absolute truth always struggling to break through from above into the world of men's minds. But once the notion of relative truth in Scripture was clearly recognized, the way was opened to a host of questions that might be asked about the conditions under which biblical books had been written and preserved down through the ages.

Henceforth the Bible, once the objectively infallible source of authority for Protestants, was now seen to be not only a body of historical information but was itself a historical product. The quality of verbal inspiration could at best be ascribed to the original autographs only, but they were lost beyond recovery. Since textual study revealed many variant readings in the manuscripts, the utmost that diligent students could accomplish was to establish the primitive text on the basis of more or less probability. This process of "lower" criticism was only a prelude to the more disturbing results of "higher" criticism. When historical study endeavored to recover dependable information about the authorship, date and provenance of a biblical book, pandemonium broke loose in the theological world.

The crest of the storm over biblical criticism was passed by the close of the nineteenth century. Liberal thought lost confidence in the infallibility of even the best attested historical records. In the process of sifting the genuine from the spurious in the biblical canon, scholars discovered that both elements were local and temporal products. Historical truth was found to be relative to the experiences and opinions of people living in a particular geographical, chronological and cultural setting. When a theologian had become genuinely historical-minded he could no longer proceed with confidence to derive from the Bible a system of doctrine suitable to all needs of the present day. Permanent validity did not necessarily inhere in a concatenation of even the best authenticated Scriptural texts. The Bible remained inspiring as a record of the religious ideals, experiences, and opinions of earnest persons who had lived in the past, but it was no longer literally inspired.

One of biblical criticism's most significant results for Christian doctrine in the late nineteenth century was the new interpretation given to the life and work of Jesus. The " liberal " view of Jesus, as it has been generally termed, was not purely a result of historical study of the Gospels, but research in this field was extensively employed to fortify and redefine a distinctive type of Christological thinking that is still widely influential in modern times. As a matter of fact its initial incentive derived from the philosophy of Kant and Hegel revised under the influence of Schleiermacher and recast by Ritschl.

Traditional theology had phrased its doctrine of Christ in terms of a duality of divine and human nature miraculously combined and attested in the Scriptural records. Since God and man were assumed to be totally different in nature, their meeting in Christ was an unprecedented and supernaturally effected phenomenon. Thus the incarnation was the unique event in the cosmic process by which salvation was made available for those who believed in the revelation and complied with the conditions therein prescribed. This theoretical Christology lost its prestige when Kant proposed to find God most truly in the sphere of moral values.

Now the divine and the human met on the ethical plane in the life of every person who obeyed the moral imperative, and Christ differed from other men only in the degree of his moral and spiritual excellence.

Schleiermacher's method of bridging the chasm between deity and humanity proved still more appealing. His thesis that the essence of all true religion is the consciousness of oneness with the divine was readily applicable to Christ, of whom it could now be said that his deity consisted in the perfection of his consciousness of unity with God. Through fellowship with Christ men acquired this same feeling of communion with the infinite. In revealing to mankind the character of his perfect religious experience Christ stimulated them to a like realization and thus became their Savior. Ritschl, while denying neither the moral nor the spiritual perfection of Jesus, added the essentially Hegelian notion of a transcendent divine purpose of which Christ was conscious and in the possession of which his deity consisted. Believers, learning through their communion with Christ to share in this purpose, become partakers in the victory that he won by means of his trust in God. Thus it was that he became their Savior. In mediating this victory Jesus had the value of God for men. The worshiping Christian community, identifying itself with the dynamic purpose that dominated the life of Jesus, found God in him.

This trend in Christological thinking, freeing religion from subordination to any specific set of dogmas or to any body of cult practices, stimulated a new interest in history. Whether one stressed the moral perfection, the spiritual sensitivity, or the clarity of the divine purpose exemplified by Jesus, the ultimate source of truth was the Bible and specifically the gospel records. Ritschl himself was rather impatient with the devotion to gospel criticism that had already begun in his day; he was content with the subjective assurance afforded by his philosophical principle. But others felt the call of the times for more objective certainty based on historically verified data. By distinguishing the genuine from the spurious in the New Testament accounts of Jesus' life and teaching, one recovered in Jesus' God-consciousness and in his moral and spiritual ideals all doctrines essential to genuine Christianity as the absolute religion for all men and all time. The result was a type of modern theology popularized, for example, in Harnack's lectures on *Das Wesen des Christentums*, published in 1900 and translated the next year into English under the title, *What is Christianity?* Probably it was one of the most generally read and influential books in circulation among moderately liberal-minded Christians during the first decade of the twentieth century. In slightly varying forms and revisions the type of thinking it presented is widely prevalent even to the present day.

The acquisition of new knowledge in the realm of physical science also had a momentous influence upon the course of Christian doctrine. Astronomers and geologists undermined long-standing traditional notions about the earth and the universe. In the light of the new physical sciences the whole scheme of biblical cosmology had to be revised. For the literalist there were only two alternatives. Either he denied the validity of science or he rejected the Bible outright and abandoned religion. In either event he retained the older authoritarian attitude, from which scientists were sometimes no more immune than were theologians. But the liberals attempted a readjustment in thinking. At first they allegorized the Bible and rephrased natural theology in an effort to harmonize traditional faith with modern scientific knowledge.

The doctrine of evolution, now promulgated as a scientific theory, saved the day for many a theologian. Originally this was a philosophical concept that had been somewhat theologized by Leibnitz, and especially by Hegel, before Charles Darwin established its vogue among biologists. The Hegelian interpretation of history, as a process by which the absolute Deity comes to self-realization in the finite sphere, had opened up a way by which God could be connected immanently with the developmental process in all nature. Evolution was only another name for God acting not merely from above but within his world, displaying his beneficent, intelligent, infinite and eternal energy. Even to posit a simian ancestry for man did not seem to cut him off so sharply from deity as was done by the older doctrine of a total depravity imposed by Adam upon his descendants. Nature was always in a state of flux, yet the process could be trusted because gradual progress toward higher levels was insured by the indwelling power of the Deity. In his Lowell Lectures on *The Ascent of Man,* given forty odd years ago, Henry Drummond clearly set forth this type of evolutionary supernaturalism. In slightly modified forms it is still widely in vogue, particularly among scientists who assume the role of apologetic theologians.

By some theologians it was felt that the doctrine of immanence, implied in this new natural theology, left the farther reaches of the religious imagination grasping at too shadowy a substance. Pushed to the extreme on the natural level it might yield a pure pantheism that made God as impersonal as the mountain or the atom, while at the other extreme infinity became a deified cipher. But most of us think so well of ourselves that we cannot be content with a God-imagery that is not modeled after the pattern of human personality. At any rate, our processes of thought, appreciation of values and sense of moral obligations are inseparably bound up with individual entities, and in the late nineteenth century individuals were growing more acutely aware of their importance and responsibilities in the concrete world of things. Inevitably some of them would turn with new zest to pursue the path of personal idealism as the most promising route to ultimate truth in religious thinking. While it was patently absurd to picture God in the physical form of a man, an absolute and transcendental will and intelligence seemed as necessary for the macrocosm of infinity as for the microcosm of finite human beings. Hence there was a disposition again to bring Christian doctrine back into the realm of metaphysics, if not by the highway of the older absolutistic thinking, at least by the closely parallel path of personal idealism. Yet the world of nature could not be totally ignored; it had to be explained from within by the aid of light from above. The doctrine of evolution seemed too firmly established to be expunged completely from the record.

On the other hand, the world of natural evolution had also to reckon with the wilful creature called *homo sapiens*. Assuming that the physical constitution of man had kept step with the progress of material evolution, would the same optimistic hypothesis hold true in the realm of ethics? And if the law of moral evolution was as inviolable as the law of gravity, would not personal ethical initiative become quiescent or anomalous? Restless activity was a conspicuous aspect of life during the latter part of the nineteenth century, and with all the good things it produced there emerged also numerous evils that sensitively religious persons could not ignore. When the theory of evolution was given consistent application to human society it created a whole series of new problems for Christian doctrine in the sphere of ethical obligations and values.

Traditional theology, both Catholic and Protestant, held out no hope for an ideal social order this side of the pearly gates. One used the evil world as a training ground for the soul preparing for heaven and was grateful that God had not permitted human society to be worse. To have attempted any fundamental alterations of one's earthly environment would have implied lack of confidence in the wisdom of God and an unpardonable interference with his affairs. This somber view had been rejected by eighteenth-century rationalists who, swinging to the opposite extreme, advocated the practical perfectibility of society by means of human intelligence and action. The French Revolution temporarily disillusioned the world by showing what the human divinity of force could and could not accomplish in the way of ideal social reconstruction. But faith in the inevitability of social advance, aided by milder forms of action, survived and flourished anew in the latter part of the nineteenth century.

Thinkers who approach their problems from the point of view of optimistic social evolution tend to find man's ethical impulses and spiritual aspirations emerging out of his experiences with his fellow men in specific environmental situations. Religion may or may not be thought essential to human progress. Those forms of social philosophy that are either tacitly irreligious or openly antireligious do not concern us at present. In the view of these thinkers the church is only a subsidiary of the social process, or is an impediment to be removed as speedily as possible. Others, who give religion a more essential place in life, find the social emphasis affecting in different ways the shaping of their Christian doctrines.

The form of philosophical thought commonly called "pragmatism," when it makes room in its system for religious ideas, seeks in some manner to root them in man's social experience and action. The logic of their procedure is essentially Kantian. Religious convictions that vindicate themselves in the course of practical living thereby attest their dependability and justify their right to acceptance. Faith, at the outset a venture, becomes, by the trial and error method so to speak, a religious conviction for which one may plausibly claim practical certainty. Doctrines are born of creative faith and purposeful action; they are never to be superimposed from without or from above, and they are liable to constant revision in the light of their workable efficiency in society's operations. The quality of permanent validity that may be ascribed to beliefs depends upon evidence of their persistence and general effectiveness in the experience of men who concern themselves with the affairs of religion.

This socio-psychological quest for truth may extend in either of two directions. When it moves toward theism it is able to rescue for faith a considerable amount of traditional doctrine restated in the light of modern knowledge. On the other hand, when human interests are chiefly emphasized, thinking tends to assume that man, as Protagoras said, is " the measure of all things "; no extra-social guaranties for religion are deemed necessary or desirable. With cheerful confidence in the inherent ability of man to effect his own salvation, the modern humanists see in religion the expression of man's struggle to realize the true, the beautiful and the good. Therefore religion is an important factor in the quest for the more abundant life of the human spirit.

The representatives of the so-called " social gospel," who for a generation or more have been much in evidence on the modern scene, show less confidence in the self-sufficiency of society but courageously undertake to build a new social order after a given Christian pattern. Since the middle of the nineteenth century social movements, especially in England and Germany, have been drifting away from organized Christianity and looking upon the church as an enemy to human welfare. Faced by this trend Christian thinkers have tried to show that this skeptical attitude quite misrepresents original and true Christianity. In order to correct the error they make Jesus either a genuine socialist, or at least the preacher of a gospel that would, if consistently applied to modern life, result in a radical reorganization of society and the church. It is thought a curious mistake to suppose that the Kingdom of God on earth consists in an assembly of redeemed individuals enjoying their personal assurance of divine favor without reference to their environing world. Salvation is to be attained, not simply or primarily by restoring individuals to harmony with God, but by first applying the principles of Jesus to the reconstruction of the social order. Otherwise even individuals cannot hope to be saved. The Kingdom of God is coming slowly but surely through the evolution of society into a Christian structure after the model prescribed by Jesus.

The confident hope of realizing more ideal cultural, political and religious conditions by means of a gradual advance to higher levels has been severely shaken in consequence of the World War. Democracy has suffered a serious set-back, international comity has been thrown out of equilibrium, economic prosperity has crumbled, race prejudice and insidious propaganda have played at will with the rational faculties of mankind, and the moral and spiritual ideals of Christianity have been openly flouted. There can no longer be the slightest doubt about the failure of liberal Christianity's recent efforts to usher in the millennium. This self-evident fact is capable of two interpretations. It may be viewed as a deferment of success beckoning one on to more strenuous endeavor in the future, or it may be taken to signify hopeless defeat rendering all further attempts of the sort utterly vain. The engine having stalled on an unusually steep grade, one abandons the course instead of changing gears and making another effort to climb the ascent.

Once again, as so often in the past, a non-rational, realistic and objectively authoritarian revival of Christian thinking has emerged as an antidote to complacent and overconfident optimism. Present-day spokesmen of this protest are well known among the group of theologians who tour — or detour — by the Barthian route. They see no hope in the exercise of man's native moral, rational and spiritual capacities; they regard this optimistic faith in his abilities to be simply an egoistic delusion. They talk much about the reality of evil in the world, but they so define God and his relation to man as to deny any form of belief in divine immanence. The social gospel, with its implied confidence in human ability to discover and pursue the purposes of Deity in history and in modern life, is emphatically rejected. There are no divine impulses resident in the spirit of man. Jesus revealed God, not by teaching man how to live righteously, but by announcing the impossibility of his living in any way that might be pleasing to Deity. Man is totally helpless until revelation impinges upon him from without, and even then it is no guiding or comforting voice but a tragic pronouncement of doom. The feeling of desperation is the only pathway to salvation, the consummation of which lies in another world beyond the confines of the human scene. All liberalism in doctrine and all efforts of modernism to harmonize religious thinking with present-day scientific knowledge and social activities are distrusted or scorned. Relativism, activism and optimism are unpardonable sins; authoritarianism, helpless resignation to a transcendental divine will, and utter despair of nature and man are the only virtuous attitudes. The liberals are accused of mere wishful thinking, for which, apparently, they are asked to substitute wishful believing.

III

In conclusion we venture a few remarks by way of retrospect and prospect. Amid the wide variety of diverse and rival types of doctrine contending for the allegiance of man today, it would seem that everyone ought to be able to find a commodity suitable to his tastes. Of making many theologies there appears to be no end, and study of them may prove a great weariness to the flesh. Perhaps you will have become so thoroughly inoculated with the pessimistic virus that the whole enterprise will seem unworthy of further effort. You may concede that the doctrinal heritage of Christendom remains a suitable exhibit for a museum of antiquities but has ceased to be of vital importance in the modern religious scene.

Not long ago a well known English novelist, speaking through one of his characters, alleged that Christianity like a passing tide has left behind on the beaches of life a promiscuous deposit of wriggling theologians, hopping and burrowing in the warm nutritious sand. Were it true that the tide has passed, never to return, one might be content to let the deceased champions of Christian opinion rest in peace, enshrouded in such virtues as may be allotted to them by the generosity of their critics. But tides have a defiant way of ebbing and rising again with a periodic regularity that refuses obedience alike to kings, prelates, philosophers and litterateurs. Theologians are a persistent species, perhaps not even subject to the law of the survival of the fittest. At any rate they are still with us and apparently their tribe is in no imminent danger of extinction.

No one genuinely interested in religion could wish this situation to be otherwise. Every feature of culture requires interpreters if it is to exert a healthful influence upon life. Religion, which is one of humanity's most persistent concerns, needs to be submitted to the scrutiny of intelligence in every new situation. Only thus can clear definition and accurate evaluation be realized. From time to time the content of Christian doctrine has to be rephrased or newly formulated in response to the most deeply felt spiritual needs and the highest standards of intelligence that the people of any given age find themselves capable of exercising. It may not be strictly true to say that religion would be better if there were more theologians, but it surely would be in a sad way if there were none. The real desideratum is an increased number of religious thinkers who will phrase their Christian doctrines in a way that will be true to the realities of life and in harmony with current knowledge.

The nature of the theologian's task subjects him to peculiar temptations. In the past he has displayed an amazing readiness to answer every question that human curiosity could ask about things finite and infinite. In leafing through classic treatises on Christian doctrine one is astounded at the range of their subject-matter. They set forth everything man wishes to know about God — his existence, his attributes and his activities in time and in eternity. The person and work of Christ are defined with reference to his pre-earthly existence, the purpose and outcome of his mission to earth and his status in the Godhead. There is a similarly comprehensive exposition of man's origin and nature, as well as of the way that he can escape from his sins and insure an eternal future reward. Moral and religious duties are explicitly defined. Often the picture includes secondary divine beings, such as angels and demons, with an explanation of the whole structure of the cosmos and a complete philosophy of history.

The theologian today finds difficulty in maintaining the profession's reputation for omniscience. While one critic blames him for pretending to know too much, another berates him for uncertainty or timidity when he admits inadequate knowledge. Nevertheless, modesty is his becoming adornment, although he may have to resist many a temptation to cast it aside. Even when he does not presume to be an oracle of infallible wisdom, the range of the faith he undertakes to expound and the assurance with which he feels impelled to speak may cause him to forget the limits of his information or the essentially tentative character of his conclusions. His honest convictions too readily take on the semblance of divine decrees. Thus he is betrayed into claiming finality for his sincere beliefs, thereby discrediting himself in the eyes of those who are equally sincere in their rejection of his opinions.

Wide diversities of opinion among Christian thinkers may on first sight seem damaging to their prestige. Even the theologians of the same generation cannot agree among themselves, while throughout the long course of history their divergences are still more striking. But this phenomenon may in reality represent a virtue rather than a defect. Only when they so far overreach themselves as to claim infallibility for their opinions, and thereby misinterpret their true function, do their disagreements become a serious liability. The quality of finality need not — in fact cannot — inhere in the candid opinions of intelligent persons thinking in terms of their distinctive types of experience and knowledge, and closely integrated with the concrete facts of life as known to them and interpreted in conformity with their personal contacts, temperaments and observations. Divergences of view may be actually an evidence of sincerity and a testimony to functional efficiency.

In spite of the charge sometimes voiced against theologians that they live in a rarefied atmosphere of their own making, it remains true that those whose work proves most significant and enduring are most substantially rooted in the realities of existence as experienced by them and their contemporaries. It is out of this matrix that orthodoxies and heterodoxies emerge. In the last analysis a doctrine proves acceptable because it yields satisfaction. Approved by the majority, or by the more influential members of a group, it is declared to be true, in contrast with the so-called false doctrine held by the less powerful minority. But even orthodoxy cannot permanently withstand the force of changing functional demands that in time may transform yesterday's error into tomorrow's truth. Too readily we blame theologians for this instability of doctrine, a condition that really inheres in circumstances over which they have no control.

The temporal and transitory character of Christian doctrine becomes still more evident when we survey its long course of development. The pages of history are bestrewn with the wreckage of discarded systems. Skirting along the shores of time, one is much impressed by the mass of doctrinal debris that litters the banks of the stream. Some crafts, launched only to be beached at the next turn in the tide, have been left to molder away with the passing of the years. Others have been refurbished in the hope that on further trial they might prove more seaworthy; or new structures have been created and christened with old names, all destined perhaps to founder in the troubled waters of future controversies. Their fitting epitaph would seem to have been penned by Tennyson: " Our little systems have their day; they have their day and cease to be."

But that is not the whole story. At least, doctrinal systems do not cease to arise. So long as men traffic in ideas — and the habit seems ineradicable — Christian doctrine will survive either in the form of old systems recast to suit current demands, or in new structures built more daringly, and we hope more wisely, by a new generation of thinkers. The incentives prompting this activity are irrepressible. They inhere within the life-process of religion and can no more be eliminated than the act of breathing in the life of our physical organism. By the same token changes also are inevitable. Thus the formulation of Christian doctrine ever remains in a fluid condition, however slow or violent its movement may be. One might liken it to an on-flowing river, sometimes sluggish, sometimes turgid, mingling in itself waters from many rivulets and accretions of earth from different soils along its banks; losing in the course of time by evaporation, seepage or deposit much that it once received and continually adding to its volume increments from fresh tributaries and new terrain.

What, then, shall we say of the future? When a historian turns prophet he invites disaster, unless he projects his vision so far into the future that his predictions can never be subjected to actual tests of verification. A decade ago a distinguished French historian of Christianity closed his book by forecasting the ultimate demise of both Catholicism and Protestantism. Likening all religions to living organisms that are nourished upon the death of their progenitors, he declared that Christianity was due to disappear by lapsing again into the eternal crucible. Although we are momentarily in a prophetic mood, we shall not strain at so far distant a scene. We are concerned only with the temporal crucible out of which Christian doctrine will have to be forged during the nearer tomorrows.

One's eyesight is poor indeed who does not perceive the seriousness of the tasks to be faced by those who will shape Christian doctrine in days to come. Our theologians are due for a period of strenuous and comprehensive thinking. The problems on which they must bring their intellectual energy to bear are multitudinous and complex. It will not suffice to fall back upon some well trodden path pursued in the past. They must be prepared to break new ground and discover new highways to the more distant horizon. Old doctrines about the church and its place in the life of the individual and in the social order demand reconsideration. The co-operation of religious forces, merely on the basis of traditional standards of faith and order, or former programs of life and work, may not prove fully adequate to the new situation. The relations of church and state, sacramental and sacerdotal doctrines, the formulation of creeds and confessions of faith, mystical experience and metaphysical speculation, are all due for a vigorous re-thinking.

Many perplexing factors are involved. New tendencies in philosophy and psychology, rapidly accumulating data in the physical and social sciences, the expansion of historical knowledge, a badly disordered society, the undermining of traditional moral standards, the upsurging of emotion in national and international life, the diminution of confidence in our long established institutions including even the church, the failure of nerve and the numbing disillusionment that have settled down upon many people — these are some of the difficulties that beset the future theologian. Religion is inseparably bound up with these cultural issues, and future framers of Christian doctrine will not easily find their way about in this confusing situation.

New modes of Christian thinking have often been engendered by reaction to chaotic conditions of life. Again the stage is set for actors with initiative and energy. The older types of rationalism, evangelism and authoritarianism are at best only temporizing expedients. The shifting of responsibility to God may for the moment ease man's psychological distress, but it will not restore order in a world that has been entrusted to the care and keeping of morally, spiritually and intellectually equipped humanity. As Paul, like many other great pioneers in religion, has perceived, man's sense of fellowship with the divine is the inspiration and not the substitute for his duty to work out his own salvation, even if with fear and trembling. For failure, desperation and despair there is but one sure remedy; this is renewed effort. The revival of a sobered and consecrated determination is the cure for a shocked and extravagant optimism.

Individual assurance and personal satisfaction are not to be denied to one whose opinions represent sincere convictions, intelligently composed and based upon such data as come within the range of one's grasp. The theologian may in all good conscience announce his convictions, strive to justify them in the eyes of his contemporaries, and seek to persuade them to accept his faith on its merits. But he must not presume to dictate unalterable opinions valid for everybody and for all time. Tolerant, enlightened and broad‚ minded thinking, combined with a persistent readiness to revise one's opinions under the impact of new knowledge, are the characteristics we demand in our future theologians. This is the essential temper of genuine liberalism and the scientific method of the nowadays much maligned modernism.

When modernism ceases to be a method of dealing with religious issues and becomes itself a dogmatic creed, then it loses its soul. This has been its fate at recurring periods in the history of Christianity. Lured by the popular yearning for finality, theologians, even when sensitive to new knowledge and concerned to make it available for religious thinking, are tempted to claim static validity for their conclusions. Indeed, their contemporaries may live long enough to discover that the valuable ideas of yesterday were not really the last word in wisdom. This nemesis pursues the modernist in every age. He is prone to substitute for the process of learning the finality of the thing learned — to abandon the highway to truth for a comfortable arbor by the side of the road. The beating heart that sustains life cannot attain to permanent vitality by ceasing the laborious efforts of palpitation. Modernism has its limitations, but the only sure cure for its defects is more modernism. Along this way lie liberty and hope for the future of Christian doctrine.

SELECTED BIBLIOGRAPHY

In the event that readers of this book should desire to pursue the
subject in more detail, it has seemed desirable to append a few bibliographical suggestions. The history of Christian doctrines has long
been a favorite theme of study, particularly among Protestants. The
habit traces back nearly four hundred years to that first monumental
history of the church known as the *Magdeburg Centuries* (published
1559–1574). In each of its thirteen volumes " De doctrina " is one of
the main topics and bulks large in each century of the history. Interest in the subject has continued to flourish, until today histories of
Christian doctrine are legion. Some of them treat the materials *in
extenso,* others are in the form of compendia, while still others single
out for presentation a particular tenet or a selected chronological area.
The standard works on the subject may be found listed in S. J. Case
(editor), *A Bibliographical Guide to the History of Christianity* (Chicago, 1931), Items 244–278; 503–509; 816–848; 936f.; 1175–1186;
1528–1533. The specific titles suggested below, taken from among
the more recent books in English, may be found useful for readers not
already familiar with the large body of literature in this field.

GENERAL WORKS

A. C. McGiffert, *A History of Christian Thought*, 2 vols. (New York, 1932–33);
    Protestant Thought before Kant (New York, 1911); *The Rise of Modern Re-
    ligious Ideas* (New York, 1915). Taken together, these three works consti-
    tute an excellent survey of the main items in Christian doctrine down to the
    opening of the present century.

. Harnack, *History of Dogma,* 7 vols. (London, 1894–1903). Translated from
    the third German edition. An elaborate and readable account ending with
    Luther; much expanded in the fourth German edition (1909–10).

. Seeberg, *Textbook of the History of Doctrines,* 2 vols. bound in one (Phila-
    delphia, 1905). Translated from the first German edition. A detailed and
    well-documented account coming down to the middle of the sixteenth century;
    considerably enlarged in the fourth German edition (1918–23).

. P. Fisher, *History of Christian Doctrine* (New York, 1896). A compact and accurate summary of the views of theological writers to the middle of the nineteenth century.

H. B. Workman, *Christian Thought to the Reformation* (New York, 1911). An epitome of selected opinions, readable and dependable.

G. G. Atkins, *The Making of the Christian Mind* (Garden City, N. Y., 1928). A popular and trustworthy survey.

S. Mathews, *The Atonement and the Social Process* (New York, 1930); and *The Growth of the Idea of God* (New York, 1931). Two important items of doctrine genetically studied from the social point of view.

LECTURE ONE

F. C. Burkitt, *Church and Gnosis: A Study of Christian Thought and Speculation in the Second Century* (Cambridge, 1932).

P. Carrington, *Christian Apologetics of the Second Century* (London, 1921).

S. J. Case, *Jesus Through the Centuries* (Chicago, 1932), Chaps. I–VIII; *Makers of Christianity from Jesus to Charlemagne* (New York, 1934), Chaps. I–IV.

Mary R. Ely, *Knowledge of God in Johannine Thought* (New York, 1925).

E. deFaye, *Origen and His Work* (New York, 1929).

E. R. Goodenough, *The Theology of Justin Martyr* (Jena, 1923).

A. C. McGiffert, *The God of the Early Christians* (New York, 1924).

A. H. McNeile, *St. Paul: His Life, Letters and Christian Doctrine* (Cambridge, 1920).

C. N. Moody, *The Mind of the Early Converts* (London, 1920).

R. B. Tollinton, *Alexandrine Teaching on the Universe* (London, 1932).

H. R. Willoughby, *Pagan Regeneration* (Chicago, 1929).

LECTURE TWO

N. H. Baynes, *Constantine the Great and the Christian Church* (London, 1931).

J. F. Bethune-Baker, *Introduction to the Early History of Christian Doctrine*, 4th edition (London, 1929).

F. C. Burkitt, *The Religion of the Manichees* (Cambridge, 1925).

A. E. Burn, *The Council of Nicea* (London, 1925).

S. J. Case, *The Social Triumph of the Ancient Church* (New York, 1933).

F. Homes Dudden, *Life and Times of St. Ambrose* (Oxford, 1935).

J. N. Figgis, *The Political Aspects of St. Augustine's 'City of God'* (New York, 1921).

H. M. Gwatkin, *Studies of Arianism*, 2d edition (Cambridge, 1900).

F. R. M. Hitchcock, *Irenaeus of Lugdunum: A Study of His Teaching* (Cambridge, 1914).

F. Loofs, *Nestorius and His Place in the History of Christian Doctrine* (Cambridge, 1914).

C. E. Raven, *Apollinarianism: An Essay on the Christology of the Early Church* (Cambridge, 1923).

W. J. Sparrow Simpson, *St. Augustine's Conversion: An Outline of His Development to the Time of His Ordination* (New York, 1930).

W. P. Tolley, *The Idea of God in the Theology of St. Augustine* (New York, 1930).

LECTURE THREE

H. Bett, *Johannes Scotus Erigena: A Study in Medieval Philosophy* (Cambridge, 1925).
T. S. R. Boase, *Boniface VIII* (London, 1933).
Cambridge Medieval History, Vol. V: *Contest of Empire and Papacy;* Vol. VI: *Victory of the Papacy* (New York, 1926–29).
M. C. D'Arcy, *Thomas Aquinas* (London, 1930).
E. H. Davenport, *The False Decretals* (Oxford, 1916).
F. Homes Dudden, *Gregory the Great: His Place in History and Thought* (London, 1905), Vol. II, pp. 285–443.
G. Krüger, *The Papacy: The Idea and its Exponents*, 2d edition (London, 1932).
A. J. MacDonald, *Berengar and the Reform of Sacramental Doctrine* (London, 1930); *Authority and Reason in the Early Middle Ages* (London, 1933).
C. H. McIlwain, *The Growth of Political Thought in the West* (New York, 1932).
J. T. McNeill, *Makers of Christianity from Alfred the Great to Schleiermacher* (New York, 1935), Chaps. I–V.
J. G. Sikes, *Peter Abailard* (Cambridge, 1932).
H. O. Taylor, *The Medieval Mind*, 2 vols., 2d edition (New York, 1914).
P. Vinogradoff, *Roman Law in Medieval Europe* (Oxford, 1929).
O. D. Watkins, *A History of Penance*, 2 vols. (London, 1920).
M. deWulf, *Philosophy and Civilization in the Middle Ages* (London, 1922).

LECTURE FOUR

A. W. Benn, *The History of English Rationalism in the Nineteenth Century*, 2 vols. (London, 1906).
H. Boehmer, *Luther and the Reformation in the Light of Modern Research* (London, 1930).
D. M. Cory, *Faustus Socinus* (Boston, 1932).
J. M. Creed and J. S. Boyssmith, *Religious Thought in the Eighteenth Century* (Cambridge, 1934).
W. C. D. Dampier-Williams, *The History of Science and its Relations with Philosophy and Religion* (New York, 1929).
A. W. Harrison, *The Beginnings of Arminianism* (London, 1926).
A. Hyma, *Erasmus and the Humanists* (New York, 1930).
B. Jarrett, *Social Theories of the Middle Ages, 1200–1500* (London, 1926).
R. M. Jones, *The Church's Debt to Heretics* (New York, 1925); *Spiritual Reformers in the Sixteenth and Seventeenth Centuries* (New York, 1914).
G. J. Jordan, *The Inner History of the Great Western Schism* (London, 1930).
J. Mackinnon, *A History of Modern Liberty* (New York, 1906).
J. T. McNeill, *Unitive Protestantism: A Study in our Religious Resources* (New York, 1930).

S. H. Mellone, *The Dawn of Modern Thought* (London, 1930).

J. M. Robertson, *A Short History of Free Thought*, 3d edition (New York, 1930).

F. Ruffini, *Religious Liberty* (New York, 1912).

P. Smith, *The Age of the Reformation* (New York, 1912).

N. L. Torrey, *Voltaire and the English Deists* (New Haven, 1930).

A. S. Turberville, *Medieval Heresy and the Inquisition* (London, 1920).

W. Walker, *John Calvin* (New York, 1906).

H. B. Workman, *John Wyclif*, 2 vols. (Oxford, 1926).

LECTURE FIVE

E. L. Allen, *Kierkegaard: His Life and Thought* (New York, 1935).

E. E. Aubrey, *Present Theological Tendencies* (New York, 1936).

C. S. Braden (editor), *Varieties of American Religion* (Chicago, 1936).

J. W. Buckham, *Progressive Religious Thought in America* (Boston, 1919).

S. J. Case, *Jesus Through the Centuries* (Chicago, 1932), Chaps. XI–XII.

G. C. Cell, *The Rediscovery of John Wesley* (New York, 1934).

G. Cross, *The Theology of Schleiermacher* (Chicago, 1911).

M. L. Edwards, *John Wesley and the Eighteenth Century* (London, 1933).

W. E. Garrison, *Intolerance* (New York, 1934).

F. C. Grant, *Frontiers of Christian Thinking* (Chicago, 1935).

S. Leslie, *The Oxford Movement, 1833 to 1933* (London, 1933).

J. Maritain, *Freedom in the Modern World* (New York, 1936).

S. Mathews, *The Gospel and the Modern Man* (New York, 1910); *The Faith of Modernism* (New York, 1924).

E. C. Moore, *An Outline of the History of Christian Thought since Kant* (New York, 1915).

W. Pauck, *Karl Barth: Prophet of a New Christianity?* (New York, 1931).

J. Y. Simpson, *Landmarks of the Struggle Between Science and Religion* (New York, 1926).

G. B. Smith, *Current Christian Thinking* (Chicago, 1928).

V. F. Storr, *The Development of English Theology in the Nineteenth Century, 1800–1860* (London, 1913).

W. W. Sweet, *The Story of Religions in America* (New York, 1930).

A. R. Vilder, *The Modernist Movement in the Catholic Church* (Cambridge, 1934).

C. C. J. Webb, *A Study of Religious Thought in England from 1850* (Oxford, 1933).

H. N. Wieman and B. E. Meland, *American Philosophies of Religion* (Chicago, 1936).

INDEX

Abelard, 109
Abraham, 17
Absolute, 29f., 167
Academics, 63
Act of Toleration of 1689, 148
Adam, 44f., 53, 144, 177
Age of Reason (Voltaire), 158
Alaric, 66
Albertus Magnus, 109
Alexandria, 3f., 19
Ambrose, 37, 59ff., 64, 81, 89, 104
America, 142, 156, 161, 170f.
Amsterdam, 147
Anabaptists, 141, 146
" Annates," 124
Anselm, 109
Apocalypticism, Jewish, 7
Apostles' Creed, 14, 24, 144
" Apostolic Tax," 123
Aquinas, Thomas, 109ff., 145
Arabian scholars, 106
Archbishop of Reims, 106
Arianism, 39, 57, 59, 66, 76
Aristotelianism, 105, 109
Aristotle, 18f., 105, 107f., 110
Arminians (Remonstrants), 141, 146
Ascent of Man, The (Drummond), 177
Asia Minor, 45
Athanasian Creed, 144
Athanasius, 58
Attila, 80
Augsburg Confession, v., 138
Augustine, 37, 59, 62–69, 73, 75, 77, 80ff., 87, 89ff., 93f., 96f., 103f., 105, 110, 134, 146
Augustus, 121
Authoritarianism, 177; in modern world, 183f.; in Roman Empire,

41f.; of sixteenth-century reformers, 143
Avignon, 120f.

Bacon, Francis, 148
Bagdad, 106
Baptism, 9, 16, 20, 24, 60, 88–95, 137
Baptists, 142
Barnabas, 7
Barth, Karl, 183
Basilica of St. Peter, 126
Baur, F. C., 172
Bayle, Pierre, 147
Berengar, 97, 109
Bishop of Poitiers, 59; of Rome, 40, 82, 85
Bishops, Roman, supremacy of, 69f., 80
Boethius, 104, 107
Bohemia, 130, 134
Bologna, University of, 178
Bonaventura, 110
Boniface VIII (1294–1303), 87, 120
Book of Acts, 8
" Brethren of the Common Life," 130

Caesar, the, 61
Calvin, 127, 132, 138, 144f.
Carthage, 63
Cassiodorus, 104
Cathari, 132
Catholic church, 44, 54, 59ff., 66–70, 73ff., 78, 81, 85; in Germany, 164
Catholicism, 65, 77, 189
Catholicism, Augustinian, 65; medieval, 82f.
Charlemagne, 81, 83, 85, 87
Chartres, 106
Christ, 1, 6–11, 19f., 25ff., 30, 33ff.,

197